Discipline in Special Education

To our wonderful wives,
the two Debbies,
With all of our love, always and forever,
Allan and Charlie

Discipline in Special Education

Allan G. Osborne, Jr.
Charles J. Russo

CORWIN
A SAGE Company

For information:

Corwin
A SAGE Company
2455 Teller Road
Thousand Oaks, California 91320
(800) 233-9936
Fax: (800) 417-2466
www.corwinpress.com

SAGE India Pvt. Ltd.
B 1/I 1 Mohan Cooperative
   Industrial Area
Mathura Road, New Delhi 110 044
India

SAGE Ltd.
1 Oliver's Yard
55 City Road
London EC1Y 1SP
United Kingdom

SAGE Asia-Pacific Pte. Ltd.
33 Pekin Street #02-01
Far East Square
Singapore 048763

Printed in the United States of America.

Library of Congress Cataloging-in-Publication Data

Osborne, Allan G.
Discipline in special education/Allan G. Osborne, Jr., Charles J. Russo.
    p. cm.
Includes bibliographical references and index.
ISBN 978-1-4129-5510-2 (cloth)
ISBN 978-1-4129-5511-9 (pbk.)
    1. Special education—United States—Administration. 2. School discipline—United States. 3. Learning disabled children—Behavior modification—United States. 4. Learning disabled children—Legal status, laws, etc.—United States. I. Russo, Charles J. II. Title.

LC3981.O725 2009
371.9—dc22   2008053029

This book is printed on acid-free paper.

09   10   11   12   13   10 9 8 7 6 5 4 3 2 1

Acquisitions Editor:	Arnis Burvikovs
Associate Editor:	Desirée A. Bartlett
Production Editor:	Cassandra Margaret Seibel
Copy Editor:	Cate Huisman
Typesetter:	C&M Digitals (P) Ltd.
Proofreader:	Susan Schon
Indexer:	Jean Casalegno
Cover Designer:	Lisa Riley
Graphic Designer:	Anthony Paular

Contents

Preface

WHY WE WROTE THIS BOOK

In 1975 Congress passed landmark legislation, originally known as the Education for All Handicapped Children Act (EHCA), that created a federal mandate for states to develop educational programs for students with disabilities. The act requires states, through local school boards and other educational agencies, to provide a free appropriate public education for all students with disabilities. Currently known as the Individuals with Disabilities Education Act (IDEA), the title that we use throughout this book for consistency, this law was initially passed, in part, in response to Congress's finding that far too many students with disabilities had been completely excluded from the educational system. Most of the students who were excluded were those who were difficult for school personnel to handle. This included students who exhibited behavior problems due to their disabilities. More than a decade after the IDEA was enacted, in 1988, the U.S. Supreme Court in *Honig v. Doe* acknowledged that one of the reasons the law was passed was to prevent school administrators from excluding students with disabilities who had behavior problems.

Ironically, none of the provisions in the original IDEA specifically addressed the discipline of special education students. Even so, a vast body of case law quickly developed as school administrators struggled with the challenge of maintaining safe school environments while meeting the mandates of the new law. Much of this case law attempted to strike a balance by allowing school officials to discipline students with disabilities without depriving them of their rights under the IDEA. It was not until 1997 that Congress inserted detailed language into the IDEA to address disciplining of students with disabilities. The IDEA's discipline provisions were modified as part of another amendment to the IDEA in 2004.

Together these two amendments codified much of the case law that had developed. More important, these modifications provided school officials with much needed guidance on how to discipline students with disabilities. The success of these amendments is evidenced by the noticeable decline in litigation over disciplinary issues since their implementation.

School officials are often heard to lament that students with disabilities are immune to the disciplinary process. This statement could not be further from the truth. The fact is that students with disabilities may be disciplined when they violate school rules. However, the process for disciplining students with disabilities is different from that used for the general population. The IDEA and its regulations have set procedures in place to ensure that the rights of students with disabilities to a free appropriate public education in the least restrictive environment are not circumvented by the disciplinary process. In other words, these procedures have been implemented to prevent school boards from excluding students who have behavior problems, as was the case prior to the enactment of the original version of the IDEA in 1975. Unfortunately, due to the long history of exclusion, the courts and Congress found it necessary to provide students with disabilities with additional protections to ensure that the disciplinary process could not be used as a subterfuge for removing them because their disabilities present unique challenges.

The purpose of this book is to provide school administrators with the knowledge needed to discipline students with disabilities properly without violating their rights under the IDEA. Although every situation is unique, a thorough knowledge of the law will help school administrators make legally correct decisions that can withstand legal challenges. In this respect, this book reviews the IDEA provisions pertinent to discipline and analyzes the case law that has developed over the years. The book has been designed to provide an exhaustive analysis of the legal requirements and suggestions on how each of the mandates can be implemented.

WHO SHOULD READ THIS BOOK

This book is intended primarily for building-level school administrators who are on the front lines of dealing with disciplinary issues on a daily basis. As such, it is specifically geared toward school principals, assistant principals, guidance counselors, and special education practitioners. It will also be useful for district-level officials, especially special education administrators, who will often be called in to assist in difficult or contentious situations. It may also be used as a supplementary text in school law courses.

As with our other books, this one is not intended to replace the advice and counsel of school board attorneys. Rather, the book is designed to make school personnel more aware of how various laws interact with the rights of individuals with disabilities in school settings. We hope that educators who understand these laws will be in a better position to implement their myriad of legal requirements and make legally correct decisions. Even so, we caution readers to consult their school board attorneys when difficult situations arise.

HOW THE BOOK IS ORGANIZED

Writing this book presented several organizational challenges. Insofar as many of the subtopics interact with each other, it was difficult to decide the order of the chapters and even the subtopics within each chapter. In some respects our decisions regarding the placement of subtopics was arbitrary. For example, many of the IDEA's procedural provisions apply to more than one type of disciplinary sanction (e.g., a provision could apply to an expulsion or to a proposed transfer to a more restrictive setting). Rather than repeat the discussions of procedural issues, we have covered them at the first appropriate opportunity and simply referred back to the original coverage when they apply to topics discussed later. Even so, some repetition of concepts was necessary to present a clear picture of the legal requirements in each of the subtopics covered. We also recognize that this book may be used as a desk reference and may not always be read cover-to-cover. For that reason, repetition is also necessary.

We also struggled with language and terms throughout the book. Recognizing that our primary audience is school personnel, we have tried to keep the use of legal terminology to a minimum. In the few instances where it has been necessary to use a legal term, we have tried to define it in context. We have also included a brief glossary of terms, acronyms, and abbreviations at the end of the book. Over the years the terminology used to identify various disabilities has changed. Again, we have made an attempt to use the terminology that is current in the field of special education. Moreover, the written opinions of many of the court cases we review in this book contain outdated terms. Rather than translate the vocabulary used by the courts, with the chance of not doing so correctly, when discussing specific cases we have used the terms found in the written decisions themselves. The result is that in some instances the terminology used may be outdated or may not be politically correct. We ask the readers' understanding that the language used is that of the courts and not ours.

The first chapter serves as an introduction to the American legal system. In including Chapter 1 we assume that many readers may not have an understanding of how the legal system works. Thus, we provide information about the various levels of our court systems. We also provide guidance on accessing and using legal materials.

Chapter 2 provides thorough information on the legal issues involved with disciplining students in general. Admittedly, the discussions in this chapter apply more to students who do not have disabilities. We included this because we think that readers will benefit from a thorough grounding in the law as it applies to students in general before delving into the intricacies of disciplinary sanctions as applied to students with disabilities. In this respect, Chapter 2 covers general issues such as suspensions, expulsions, and due process along with more specialized topics such as locker searches.

The third chapter presents an overview of the three major laws affecting special education: the IDEA, Section 504 of the Rehabilitation Act, and the Americans with Disabilities Act. Chapter 3 also includes a review of the case law that developed prior to the inclusion of disciplinary provisions in the IDEA. We provide this "history lesson" with the knowledge that we need to understand where we have been before we can move forward. Insofar as the current disciplinary sections of the IDEA are largely based on this prior case law, this history helps us to understand how the statutory mandates should be implemented.

Chapter 4 outlines the procedures school officials must follow when contemplating the removal of students with disabilities from the general education setting for disciplinary purposes. In addition to discussing suspensions and expulsions, Chapter 4 provides detailed information about functional behavioral assessments, behavior intervention plans, and determining whether students' misbehavior is a manifestation of their disabilities, an important distinction.

The fifth chapter presents information about how school administrators can transfer students with disabilities to other, possibly more restrictive, educational settings. Chapter 5 includes a discussion about the IDEA's normal change in placement procedures along with the special circumstances where students can be moved to interim alternative educational settings or even be barred from attending their former placements altogether.

In the sixth chapter we provide information about other disciplinary issues that arise in the schools. Chapter 6 begins with a review of litigation concerning minor disciplinary practices that may be used with special education students. The chapter also reviews the related subjects of the rights of students not yet identified as having disabilities and those who are no longer receiving services under an individualized education program (IEP). Chapter 6 closes with a discussion of the interaction between schools and the juvenile justice system.

The seventh and final chapter summarizes the major points made in the book and provides readers with some practical advice on meeting the various legal requirements. Chapter 7 also contains sample forms that may be used in the disciplinary process.

In the resources at the end of the book we have reproduced the applicable disciplinary provisions of the IDEA from the *United States Code* and the *Code of Federal Regulations*. We have also included an edited version of the U.S. Supreme Court's opinion in *Honig v. Doe*, the Court's first and, to date, only decision concerned with disciplining students with disabilities. A list of Web sites that will provide additional information on school law in general and a glossary are also included in the resources.

Acknowledgments

We could not have written this book without the encouragement, support, advice, and assistance of many friends, colleagues, and family members. Even though it is impossible to acknowledge all who have influenced us in some way and so contributed to this book, we would at the very least like to extend our gratitude to those who have had the greatest impact in our lives. This group includes all who have contributed to our knowledge and understanding of the subject matter of this book, most notably our many friends and colleagues who are members of the Education Law Association. These professionals have not only consistently shared their knowledge with us but also, more important, provided constructive criticism and constantly challenged our thinking. We also include our graduate students who, as educational practitioners, have kept us abreast of the problems they face daily in their schools.

We are also most fortunate to work with a group of professionals who understand the importance of our work and provide us with the support and resources to continue our research. The contributions of many colleagues from the Quincy Public Schools and University of Dayton can never be adequately acknowledged.

I (Allan Osborne) especially thank Superintendent Richard DeCristofaro and the entire administrative team of the Quincy Public Schools for all of their encouragement and support during my years in that school system. In that respect I want to extend a special thank you to my good friends and former colleagues, Dennis Carini and Carol Shiffer, for their unending support and encouragement, along with their unlimited patience when I bounced ideas off them. My appreciation for their friendship can never be adequately acknowledged. Shortly before undertaking this book I retired after many years as a teacher and administrator in the Quincy Public Schools. Most recently I served as the Principal of the Snug Harbor Community School. I would like to extend a very sincere and warm thank you to the faculty, parents, and students of that school for close to two and a half decades of rewards and inspiration. Special thanks are extended to my support team of Bob Limoncelli, Chris Karaska, and Amy Carey-Shinney, without whom I would not have been successful. A school administrator is no better than his or her secretarial staff, and I was very fortunate to have the best. Much appreciation and love is extended to Angie Priscella and Jeanne Furlong for their loyalty and for always being there to support me.

Finally, I wish to thank two great neighbors, Ed Hacker and Pat Clark, for their friendship during the past 25 years. My wife and I could not ask for better neighbors and their constant support and encouragement are very much valued. We look forward to many more enjoyable evenings with them in the gazebo.

In the School of Education and Allied Professions at the University of Dayton, I (Charlie Russo) would like to express my thanks to Rev. Joseph D. Massucci, Chair of the Department of Educational Leadership; Dr. Thomas J. Lasley II, Dean; and Dr. Dan Raisch, Associate Dean, for their ongoing support and friendship. I also extend a special note of thanks to my assistant Ms. Elizabeth Pearn for her valuable assistance in helping to process the manuscript, to Ms. Colleen Wildenhaus for assistance in proofreading the final manuscript, and to Mrs. Ann Raney of the Curriculum Materials Center for the many times that she has helped me to find information for this book and many other projects.

We would both like to thank our acquisitions editor at Corwin, Arnis Burvikovs, our production editor Cassandra Seibel, and associate editor Desiree Bartlett for their support as we conceptualized, wrote, and revised this book. We especially thank Cate Huisman whose copyediting skills greatly improved this book. It is a pleasure working with such outstanding professionals and their colleagues at Corwin. They certainly helped to make our jobs easier. We also wish to thank the reviewers who provided helpful comments on an earlier draft of this book. Many of their suggestions have been incorporated into the final product.

On a more personal note, we both extend our appreciation to our late parents, Allan G. and Ruth L. Osborne and James J. and Helen J. Russo. We can never adequately express our gratitude to our parents for the profound influences that they have had on our lives.

I (Charlie Russo) also extend a special note of thanks and appreciation to my two wonderful children, Emily Rebecca and David Peter, and to David's wife Li Hong. The bright and inquisitive children that my wife Debbie and I had the pleasure of raising have grown to be wonderful young adults who provide us both with a constant source of inspiration and love.

Our wonderful wives, affectionately known as the two Debbies, have been the major influence in our lives and professional careers. Our best friends, they encourage us to write, show great patience as we ramble on endlessly about litigation in special education, and understand when we must spend countless hours working on a manuscript. We would not be able to do all that we do if it were not for their constant love and support. Thus, as we do with all of our work, we dedicate this book to them with all of our love.

—A. G. O.

—C. J. R.

PUBLISHER'S ACKNOWLEDGMENTS

Corwin gratefully acknowledges the contributions of the following individuals:

Diane Adreon
Associate Director, Center for Autism and Related Disabilities
University of Miami
Coral Gables, FL

Laurie Emery
Principal
Old Vail Middle School
Vail, AZ

Jo-Anne Goldberg
Director, Special Education
Mainland Regional High School
Linwood, NJ

Barb Keating
Principal
F. W. Howay Community School
New Westminster, BC, Canada

Bill Morgan
Special Education Coordinator
Judson Independent School District
San Antonio, TX

About the Authors

Allan G. Osborne, Jr., EdD, is the former principal of the Snug Harbor Community School in Quincy, Massachusetts. Retired after 34 years as a special education teacher and school administrator, he is currently serving as a consultant to the College of Education at Kutztown University in Pennsylvania. He received his doctorate in educational leadership from Boston College. Allan Osborne has authored or coauthored numerous articles, monographs, textbooks, and textbook chapters on special education law, along with textbooks on other aspects of special education. A past president of the Education Law Association (ELA) and 2008 recipient of their McGhehey Award for lifetime achievement and service, he has been a frequent presenter at ELA conferences and writes the "Students With Disabilities" chapter of the *Yearbook of Education Law,* which is published by ELA. Allan Osborne is on the editorial advisory committee of *West's Education Law Reporter* and is coeditor of the "Education Law Into Practice" section of that journal. He also serves as an editorial consultant for many other publications in education law, administration, and special education.

Charles J. Russo, JD, EdD, is the Joseph Panzer Chair in Education in the School of Education and Allied Professions and Adjunct Professor in the School of Law at the University of Dayton, Ohio. The 1998–1999 president of the Education Law Association and 2002 recipient of its McGhehey (Lifetime Achievement) Award, he is the author of almost 200 articles in peer-reviewed journals and the author, coauthor, editor, or coeditor of 35 books. He has been the editor of the *Yearbook of Education Law* for the Education Law Association since 1995 and has written or coauthored almost 700 publications; he is also the editor of two academic journals and serves as a member of more than a dozen editorial boards. Russo has spoken and taught extensively on issues in Education Law in the United States and in twenty-two other nations on all six inhabited continents. In recognition of his work in Education Law in countries outside the United States, he received an honorary PhD from Potchefstroom University, now the Potchefstroom Campus of North-West University, in Potchefstroom, South Africa, in May of 2004.

OTHER CORWIN BOOKS
BY OSBORNE AND RUSSO

Special Education and the Law: A Guide for Practitioners, Second Edition

Essential Concepts and School-Based Cases in Special Education Law

Section 504 and the ADA

1

Education and the American Legal System

Key Concepts in This Chapter

♦ Sources of Law

♦ Court System

♦ Legal Resources

♦ Legal References and Citations

INTRODUCTION

Education in the United States is predominantly a state function under the Tenth Amendment of the federal Constitution, which states that "the powers not delegated to the United States by the Constitution, nor prohibited by it to the States, are reserved to the States respectively, or to the people." Even so, many federal laws currently affect the day-to-day operations of public schools. Before any presentation of the legal issues that arise in public education can occur, it is essential for readers to understand the legal framework under which American schools operate on both the federal and state levels. Accordingly, this introductory chapter examines the sources and types of laws in the American legal system while also presenting information on how these laws influence the daily operations of public schools. In addition, the chapter provides an overview of the American court systems and a basic primer on using and understanding legal resources and references.

SOURCES OF LAW

There are four sources of law in the United States: constitutions, statutes, regulations, and judicial decisions. These sources exist at both the federal and state levels. A constitution is the fundamental law of a nation or state (Garner, 2004). A statute is an act of the legislative body, a law enacted by Congress or a state legislature (Garner, 2004). All statutes, whether federal or state, must be consistent with the controlling constitutions within their respective jurisdictions. Most statutes are accompanied by implementing regulations or guidelines issued by the agencies responsible for their execution and enforcement. Regulations are usually more specific than the statutes they are designed to implement, because they interpret legislative intent as to how laws should work in practice. Moreover, the frequent opinions issued by the federal and state courts interpreting the constitutions, statutes, and regulations compose a body of law known as case, judge-made, or common law.

> "The powers not delegated to the United States by the Constitution, nor prohibited by it to the States, are reserved to the States respectively, or to the people."
>
> *—U.S. Constitution,*
> *Tenth Amendment*

Case law, which occupies a central role in this, or any, law book, provides further insight into how constitutions, statutes, and regulations should be applied to factual situations (Russo, 2005). Case law relies greatly on the notion of binding precedent, that is, the principle that a ruling of the highest court in a jurisdiction is binding on all lower courts in that jurisdiction. Even though cases from other jurisdictions have no binding effect on courts outside of their jurisdictions, they are referred to as persuasive precedent. In other words, decisions of courts in one jurisdiction are of no legal effect in other jurisdictions but may have some influence on how courts interpret the laws of their states.

Constitutions

The Constitution of the United States is the law of the land. Accordingly, all federal statutes and regulations, state constitutions, state laws and regulations, and ordinances of local governmental bodies, including school boards, are subject to the Constitution as it has been interpreted by the U.S. Supreme Court and other courts. In fact, very few sections of the U.S. Constitution are implicated in education-related litigation. For the most part, the sections of the Constitution that impact most dramatically on the operation of the schools are those protecting individual rights, such as the First, Fourth, Fifth, and Fourteenth Amendments.

In the same way, state constitutions are the supreme law in their respective jurisdictions and are the measure by which all of their state's statutes, regulations, and ordinances are judged. State constitutions typically deal with many of the same matters as the U.S. Constitution and may provide even greater protection than their federal counterpart.

Statutes and Regulations

As noted, under the Tenth Amendment to the Constitution, education is reserved to the States (*Epperson v. State of Arkansas,* 1968). Even so, Congress has the power to enact laws under the general welfare clause of Article I, Section 8 of the Constitution by offering funds for purposes that it believes will serve the public good. For example, Congress has enacted a series of statutes, such as the Civil Rights Act of 1964 (2006) that subject public school systems to its antidiscrimination in employment provisions.

When federal statutes make funds available to state and local governments, the money is conditioned on the governments' acceptance of explicit requirements for its use. As discussed below, when states accept federal funds, school officials are bound by whatever conditions Congress has attached to the legislation associated with the funds. If challenged, governmental agencies must satisfy federal courts that those conditions pass constitutional muster. In 1987, for instance, Congress expanded its authority by defining a "program or activity" as encompassing "all of the operations of [an entity] any part of which is extended Federal financial assistance" (Civil Rights Restoration Act of 1987, 2006). This broad general prohibition covers "race, color or national origin," (42 U.S.C. § 2000d) "sex," (20 U.S.C. § 1681) and "otherwise qualified handicapped individuals," (29 U.S.C. § 794), categories that have become increasingly important in school settings. By way of illustration, in order to receive funding for special education under the Individuals With Disabilities Education Act (2006), states, typically through state and local educational agencies (or school boards), must develop detailed procedures to identify and assess children with disabilities before offering each qualified student a free appropriate public education in the least restrictive environment.

Another recent example of federal involvement in education, the No Child Left Behind Act (NCLB, 2006), was enacted by Congress in 2002.

> The Constitution of the United States is the law of the land. Accordingly, all federal statutes and regulations, state constitutions, state laws and regulations, and ordinances of local governmental bodies, including school boards, are subject to the Constitution as it has been interpreted by the U.S. Supreme Court and other courts.

> When federal statutes make funds available to state and local governments, the money is conditioned on the governments' acceptance of explicit requirements for its use. When states accept federal funds, school officials are bound by whatever conditions Congress has attached to the legislation associated with the funds.

States receiving federal financial assistance under the NCLB must take steps to improve academic achievement among students who are economically disadvantaged; assist in preparing, training, and recruiting "highly qualified" staff; provide improved language instruction for children of limited English proficiency; make school systems accountable for student achievement, particularly by imposing standards for annual yearly progress for students and districts; require school systems to rely on teaching methods that are research based and that have been proven effective; and afford parents better choices while creating innovative educational programs, especially if local school systems are unresponsive to their needs.

> Regulations issued by the federal Department of Education and other administrative agencies give the executive branch the means to implement statutes by carrying out their full effect.

Regulations issued by the federal Department of Education and other administrative agencies give the executive branch the means to implement statutes by carrying out their full effect. Put another way, while statutes set broad legislative parameters, regulations allow administrative agencies to provide details to satisfy the requirements of the law. By way of illustration, while statutes set the number of days that children must attend school to satisfy state compulsory attendance laws, regulations fill in such details as how long class days should be and what subjects students must study. Regulations generally carry the full force of the law and are presumptively valid unless or until such times as courts strike them down as conflicting with the underlying legislation.

Most of the statutes impacting public schools come from state legislatures. While state legislatures are subject to the limitations of federal law and of state constitutions, they are relatively free to establish their own systems of education. The law is well settled that state and local boards of education, administrators, and teachers have the authority to adopt and enforce reasonable rules and regulations to ensure the smooth operation and management of schools. Rules and regulations are subject to the same constitutional limitations as statutes passed by legislative bodies. Thus, if it is unconstitutional for Congress or state legislatures to enact laws violating the free speech rights of children, it is also impermissible for teachers to do so by creating rules that apply only in their classrooms. Put another way, while teachers are certainly free to institute their own classroom rules, they, too, must act in a manner that is consistent with the Constitution. It is also significant to note that legislation or rule-making on any level, whether federal or state, cannot conflict with a higher authority.

Common Law

The function of the courts is to interpret the law. When there is no codified law, or if statutes or regulations are unclear, courts apply common law. Common law is basically judge-made law, meaning that courts may adjust the law to new or changing circumstances. The collective decisions of the courts make up the body of common law. When disputes involve legislation, the task of the courts is to discover, as best they can, the intent of the legislative bodies that enacted statutes. To the degree that judicial decrees establish precedent, they have considerable weight in terms of providing guidance on how statutes and regulations are to be applied to everyday situations.

> Common law is basically judge-made law, meaning that the courts may adjust the law to new or changing circumstances. The collective decisions of the courts make up the body of common law.

Court Systems

The federal court system and most state judicial systems have three levels. The lowest level in the federal system consists of trial courts that are known as federal district courts. Each state has at least one federal district court, while larger states, such as California and New York, may have as many as four. District courts are the basic triers of fact in legal disputes. These trial courts review evidence and render decisions based on the evidence presented by the parties to disputes. Depending on the situation, trial courts may review the record of any administrative hearings that have been held, hear additional evidence, and/or hear the testimony of witnesses.

> The federal court system and most state judicial systems have three levels.

Parties that are dissatisfied with the decisions of trial courts may appeal to the federal circuit court of appeals within which their states are located. For example, a decision issued by a federal trial court in New York would be appealed to the Second Circuit, which, in addition to New York, consists of the states of Connecticut and Vermont. There are 13 federal judicial circuits in the United States. The circuits were created for judicial and administrative ease and convenience so that parties seeking to appeal judgments with which they disagree would not have to travel too far from home to do so. The map in Figure 1.1 shows the location of the federal circuits and the states that fall within each circuit.

Individuals who are still dissatisfied with the judgments of the circuit courts may appeal to the U.S. Supreme Court. Owing to the sheer volume of cases appealed, the Supreme Court accepts less than one percent of the approximately 8,000 cases annually in which parties seek further review. Cases typically reach the Court in requests for a writ of *certiorari*, which literally means "to be informed of." When the Supreme Court agrees to hear an appeal, it grants a writ of *certiorari*. At least four of the nine Justices must vote to grant *certiorari* in order for a case to be heard. Denying a writ of

Figure 1.1 Federal Circuit Courts of Appeal

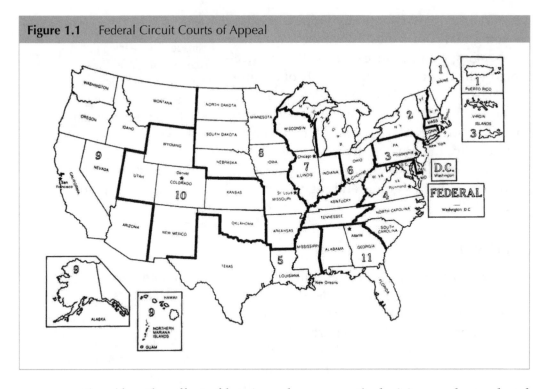

certiorari has the effect of leaving a lower court's decision unchanged and is of no precedential value.

The court systems in each of the 50 states and various territories are arranged in an organizational fashion that is similar to the federal format except that the names of the courts vary. In most states, there are three levels of courts: trial courts, intermediate appellate courts, and courts of last resort. Readers are cautioned to pay particular attention to the names of state courts, as they are not consistent from state to state. For example, people generally think of a supreme court as being the highest court. However, in New York, the trial court is known as the Supreme Court, the intermediate level is named the Supreme Court Appellate Division, while the state's high court is called the Court of Appeals, typically the name for intermediate appellate courts in most jurisdictions.

When courts render their judgments, their opinions are binding only within their jurisdictions. In other words, a judgment of the federal trial court for Rhode Island is binding only in Rhode Island. The federal trial court in Maine, which is in the same federal circuit, may find a decision of the Rhode Island court persuasive, but it is not bound by its order. Nonetheless, a ruling of the First Circuit Court of Appeals is binding on all states within its jurisdiction, and lower courts in Maine, Massachusetts, New Hampshire, Rhode Island, and Puerto Rico must rule consistently.

> When courts render their judgments, their opinions are binding only within their jurisdictions.

A decision by the Supreme Court of the United States is, of course, enforceable in all 50 states and American territories.

Readers should keep in mind that a court's jurisdiction can refer to either the types of cases that it can hear or to the geographic area over which it has authority. The preceding paragraph referred to jurisdiction by geographic area. At the same time, courts are typically limited by the type of jurisdiction, or ability to hear cases, with which they are empowered. For example, as discussed in a bit more detail in the next paragraph, trial courts typically have jurisdiction over cases that have yet to be tried, while the judicial authority of appellate courts is usually restricted to cases that have already proceeded through at least one level of judicial review.

As indicated earlier, the complex American court systems operate at both the federal and state levels. The most common arrangement of these systems is a three-tiered organization with trial courts, intermediate appellate courts, and courts of last resort, most commonly named supreme courts. Trial courts have general jurisdiction, so that there are few limits on the types of cases that they may hear. Trial courts hear the facts behind the dispute and apply the law to the circumstances. Trial courts are generally presided over by a single judge or justice. Intermediate courts, generally known as appellate courts or courts of appeal, review cases when a party is dissatisfied with the decision of the lower court. Appellate courts are not triers of fact but, rather, review lower courts' application of the law. In rare cases an appellate court may reject a lower court's interpretation of the facts of a case if it is convinced that the lower court's interpretation was clearly erroneous. Appellate courts usually consist of a panel of judges. For example, at the federal level appeals are heard by a panel of three judges. Finally, issues may be appealed to a court of last resort. At the federal level this is the Supreme Court. The Supreme Court has discretion to review rulings of lower federal courts and state high courts that involve federal constitutional, statutory, or regulatory issues.

Insofar as education is a state function and federal courts exist for federal matters, most disputes involving education are resolved by state courts. Unless there is a substantial federal question, such as a disagreement over a provision in the U.S. Constitution, a federal statute, or a federal regulation, cases must be tried in state courts. If a substantial federal question is involved with a state question, a dispute may be litigated either in a state or federal court. When federal courts examine cases involving both state and federal law, they must follow interpretations of state law made by the state courts within which they sit. Special education disputes provide a good example of cases that frequently have mixed questions of federal and state law. To the extent that special education is governed by state laws as well as federal laws, claims are often brought on the basis of both sets of statutes. Final due process hearing decisions may be appealed to either the federal or state courts, but the vast majority of published opinions come from the federal courts.

Legal Resources and References

Federal statutes appear in the United States Code (U.S.C.), the official version, or the United State Code Annotated (U.S.C.A.), published by West Publishing Company. Agency regulations are published in the Code of Federal Regulations (C.F.R.). Copies of education statutes and regulations can be downloaded via links on the U.S. Department of Education's Web site. Legal materials are also available online from a variety of sources, most notably WestLaw and LexisNexis. State laws and regulations are commonly available online from the Web sites of their states. Appendix D provides a list of Web sites on which legal materials can be found.

The written opinions of most courts are generally available in a variety of published formats. The official versions of U.S. Supreme Court opinions are found in the *United States Reports,* abbreviated U.S. The same opinions, with additional research aids, are published in the *Supreme Court Reporter* (S. Ct.) and the *Lawyer's Edition,* now in its second series (L. Ed.2d). Opinions issued by the federal circuit courts of appeal are located in the *Federal Reporter,* currently in its third series (F.3d), while federal district court decisions are published in the *Federal Supplement,* presently in its second series (F. Supp.2d). State court cases are published in a variety of publications, most notably West's *National Reporter* system, which divides the country up into seven regions: Atlantic, North Eastern, North Western, Pacific, South Eastern, South Western, and Southern. Most education-related cases are also republished in *West's Education Law Reporter.*

> The written opinions of most courts are generally available in a variety of published formats.

Before being published in hardbound volumes, most decisions are released in what are known as slip opinions, a variety of loose-leaf services, and electronic sources. There are also many commercial services available that publish decisions in a specialized area. For example, special education court decisions, as well as due process hearing decisions, are reproduced in a loose-leaf format in the *Individuals With Disabilities Education Law Reporter* (IDELR) published by LRP Publications.

UNDERSTANDING LEGAL CITATIONS

As complicated as they may seem to readers who are unfamiliar with them, since legal citations are fairly easy to read once one understands the format, this brief description of how they work should help put the minds of some readers at ease. Most citations begin with a number followed by an abbreviation and another number. The first number indicates the volume in which

> ...legal citations are fairly easy to read once one understands the format....

the case, statute, or regulation is located, and it is followed by the abbreviation of the book or series in which the material may be found. The second number indicates the page on which a case begins or the section number of a statute or regulation. For references to judicial opinions, the last part of a citation provides the name of the court, for lower court cases, and the year in which the dispute was resolved. For example, the citation for *Farrin v. Maine School Administrative District No. 59,* 165 F. Supp.2d 37 (D. Me. 2001) can be located in volume 165 of the *Federal Supplement* second series beginning on page 37. The case was decided by the District Court for the District of Maine in 2001. Similarly, the citation for the Individuals with Disabilities Education Act, 20 U.S.C. § 1400–1482 (2006) can be found in Volume 20 of the United States Code beginning with Section 1400 and continuing through Section 1482. The latest official version of the United States Code was published in 2006. Statutes are always cited to the most recent publication of the code, not the year the particular statute was passed.

SUMMARY

As an entity subject to laws and regulations, our public educational institutions must work within the American legal system. Although education is generally considered to be a function of the states, during the past several decades the federal government has passed a number of laws that have a direct impact on the day-to-day operation of our public schools. In addition, many other laws, such as civil rights laws, which were passed for the general welfare, have implications for schools. Thus, school administrators need to be familiar with a myriad of legal requirements.

The American legal system is one of constitutions, statutes, regulations, and court decisions. Collectively, all of these make up the law under which school systems operate. Although it may appear to be complex, educators can find a plethora of legal resources at their fingertips once they understand how to access and use legal references.

This chapter has provided a basic primer on the American legal system for readers who do not have an extensive background in this area. Those who are interested in more comprehensive information on legal research may wish to consult *Research Methods for Studying Legal Issues in Education,* edited by Steve Permuth and Ralph Mawdsley and published by the

Education Law Association. *User's Guide to The Bluebook* (2006) by Alan L. Dworsky is an excellent quick resource for legal citations. The law is constantly evolving. Thus, educators who are in positions that require knowledge of the law must keep constantly updated.

RECOMMENDATIONS FOR PRACTITIONERS

- Attend local, state, and national conferences and workshops on legal issues to keep abreast of new developments. Share handouts with all staff.
- Subscribe to one of many monthly newsletters that provide updates on education law. LRP Publications is one publisher of such newsletters. Prepare summaries of new developments and provide them to all staff.
- Subscribe to an education newspaper such as *Education Week.*
- Read law review articles such as those found in *West's Education Law Reporter* and the *Journal of Law and Education.*
- Join professional organizations that regularly provide updated legal information. The Education Law Association is the premier source of information on education law. The Council for Exceptional Children, one of the leading professional organizations in special education, provides updates on new legislation and court decisions in the field.
- Purchase new editions of texts on education law topics. Make these available to all staff in a professional library.
- Enroll in or audit courses on school law at local colleges and universities.
- Invite the school board's legal counsel or experts on school law to present professional development workshops in your school system for all staff.

WHAT'S NEXT

The second chapter provides information about the legal requirements regarding discipline in general. It includes an overview of the due process safeguards school administrators must provide to all students prior to implementing any serious disciplinary consequences. The chapter also reviews basic student rights. Subsequent chapters focus specifically on disciplining students with disabilities and the additional procedures that educators must implement in this regard.

REFERENCES

Civil Rights Act of 1964, 42 U.S.C. § 2000e–2a (2006).

Civil Rights Restoration Act of 1987, 20 U.S.C. § 1687 (2006).

Dworsky, A. L. (2006). *User's guide to the Bluebook.* Buffalo, NY: William S. Hein.

Epperson v. State of Arkansas, 393 U.S. 97 (1968).

Garner, B. A. (2004). *Black's law dictionary* (8th ed.). St. Paul, MN: Thompson West.

Individuals with Disabilities Education Act (IDEA), 20 U.S.C. §§ 1400–1482 (2006).

No Child Left Behind Act (NCLB), 20 U.S.C. §§ 6301–7941 (2006).

Permuth, S., & Mawdsley, R. (2006). *Research methods for studying legal issues in education.* Dayton, OH: Education Law Association.

Russo, C. J. (2005). In the eye of the beholder: The Supreme Court, judicial activism, and judicial restraint. *School Business Affairs, 71*(8), 47–50.

United States Code (U.S.C.), as cited.

2 Student Discipline

INTRODUCTION

Honig v. Doe (*Honig*, 1988) is the Supreme Court's only case addressing the disciplining of students with disabilities under the Individuals with Disabilities Education Act (IDEA, 2006) and its regulations. In *Honig* the Court ruled that students whose misbehavior is not a manifestation of their disabilities can be disciplined in the same way as their peers who are not disabled. Under *Honig* and the IDEA, students with disabilities can be suspended for up to 10 school days in the same manner as peers who are not disabled.

In light of the broad array of issues involving student discipline, this chapter is divided into three major sections addressing student rights and school punishments, due process, and the Fourth Amendment rights of students; this last section is further subdivided to examine drug testing and searches of students and their property.

STUDENT RIGHTS AND SCHOOL PUNISHMENTS

It is well settled that educational officials have the authority to adopt rules to discipline students for misbehavior, regardless of whether it occurred in or out of school (*Fuller ex rel. Fuller v. Decatur Public School Board of Education School District 61*, 2001), that threatens their ability to maintain safe and orderly learning environments. In imposing discipline, as well as in a myriad of other aspects of their daily duties, educational officials should keep two important concepts in mind: due process and equal protection. As to due process, even if school rules are not written, students may be disciplined for breaking clearly defined rules (*Bunger v. Iowa High School Athletic Association*, 1972) that they knew or reasonably should have known, as long as punishments are proportionate to their offenses.

> It is well settled that educational officials have the authority to adopt rules to discipline students for misbehavior, regardless of whether it occurred in or out of school....

Two important conditions are associated with discipline. First, in order to satisfy due process, educators must not only impose punishments that are appropriate to student offenses but must also provide the offending students with the appropriate level of procedural due process. Second, in satisfying equal protection, educators must do all that they can to treat similarly situated students in the same way. In one such example, a federal trial court in Iowa held that school officials violated the equal protection rights of a female high school student athlete when they disciplined her more harshly for smoking a cigarette in public than they disciplined males who violated comparable team training rules in an admittedly different sport (*Schultzen v. Woodbury Central Community School District*, 2002).

It is crucial to keep in mind that when Congress enacted the IDEA, it conferred additional rights on students with disabilities. To this end, when the parents of students in regular education complain that their children receive different punishments than peers with disabilities, even if the latter initiated altercations, educators should explain that this is the way that the law operates inasmuch as Congress conferred additional rights on students with disabilities when it enacted the IDEA. Moreover, school officials will not have violated the equal protection rights of students who do not have disabilities in such disciplinary situations, because Congress decided that since the two groups of students are not similar, they can be treated differently.

When students are punished for their infractions, the burden is ordinarily on them and their parents to demonstrate that they have been treated unfairly. Of course, if students are subjected to more invasive forms of discipline such as locker searches or drug testing, then the courts typically require school officials to justify their actions.

Just as when dealing with the establishment of school rules, the courts acknowledge that educational officials must apply discretion when disciplining students who break those rules. As noted earlier, as long as discipline policies and procedures satisfy due process, courts usually uphold the actions of educators as long as they are not arbitrary, capricious, or unreasonable. Moreover, when educators discipline students, courts have taken into account factors such as students' sex, age, and size along with their mental, emotional, and/or physical conditions, especially when dealing with students with disabilities. Even so, courts generally do not require officials to provide students with the same level of due process as defendants are entitled to in criminal cases (*Wood v. Strickland*, 1975).

Turning to specific forms of punishments, the Third (*S. M. ex rel. L. G. v. Lakeland School District*, 2002) and Eighth (*Costello v. Mitchell Public School District 79*, 2001) Circuits agreed with the general rule that teachers may verbally reprimand students as long as their comments are not disparaging or malicious (*Wexell v. Scott*, 1971). In fact, the Montana Supreme Court went so far as to declare that a teacher's calling a student, who was slumped over in her chair and not paying attention, a "slob" did not warrant dismissal (*Trustees of Lincoln County School District No. 13, Eureka v. Holden*, 1988).

Courts have upheld such punishments as being adjudicated delinquent for threatening a teacher (*In re J. H.*, 2002) or causing a disruption in school (*M. C. v. State*, 1997); being charged with making a false fire-alarm report at school (*In re C. R. K.*, 2001); being disciplined for making obscene remarks to a teacher (*In Interest of D. A. D.*, 1997); being given a zero for the first offense of plagiarism on an assignment (*Zellman ex rel. M. Z. v. Independent School District No. 2758*, 1999); being dismissed from a marching band for missing a performance (*Mazevski v. Horseheads Central School District*, 1997); and being seated at an isolated desk for being disruptive (*Cole by Cole v. Greenfield-Central Community Schools*, 1986).

Perhaps the most controversial form of in-school discipline is corporal punishment, a practice that is still used in 22 states (Randall, 2008). Corporal punishment is noteworthy, because it may come into play when educators seek to impose aversive discipline on students who are in special education placements (Zirkel, 2002). In a dispute in which it did not reach the merits of the underlying claim, meaning that it was disposed of solely on procedural grounds, the Supreme Court summarily upheld an opinion of a federal trial court dealing with corporal punishment (*Baker v. Owen*, 1975a, 1975b). The Justices refused to disturb the order of a federal trial court in North Carolina that parental disapproval of corporal punishment notwithstanding, a board policy allowing the practice to be employed on students was constitutional.

The only case in which the Supreme Court heard a dispute over corporal punishment on the merits was *Ingraham v. Wright* (1977). The Court pointed out that corporal punishment was not per se unconstitutional, since the Eighth Amendment's prohibition against cruel and unusual punishments was designed to protect those guilty of crimes and did not apply to paddling students in order to preserve discipline. Even so, as reflected by cases from the Fourth (*Hall v. Tawney*, 1980; *Meeker v. Edmundson*, 2005), Tenth (*Garcia v. Miera*, 1987), and Eleventh (*Neal v. Fulton County Board of Education*, 2000) Circuits, students can proceed with substantive due process claims where punishments are "so brutal, demeaning, and harmful as literally to shock the conscience of a court" (*Hall v. Tawney*, 1980, p. 613).

As demonstrated by litigation from the Second (*Smith ex rel. Smith v. Half Hollow Hills Central School District*, 2002), Third (*Gottlieb ex rel. Calabria v. Laurel Highlands School District*, 2001), and Seventh (*Wallace by Wallace v. Batavia School District 101*, 1995) Circuits, there are times when teachers may have to use force to remove disruptive students. In such a case from Illinois, the Seventh Circuit specified that when a teacher in Illinois grabbed a student by her wrist and elbow to escort her from a classroom, he did not violate her rights to substantive due process amounting to corporal punishment. Similarly, a variety of federal and state courts agree that teachers did not commit corporal punishment where they paddled a child on the buttocks (*Fox v. Cleveland*, 2001), restrained a child with Asperger syndrome (*Brown ex rel. Brown v. Ramsey*, 2000), grabbed the arm of a student who was attempting to retrieve a shirt and pulled him toward a door (*Widdoes v. Detroit Public Schools*, 2000), and twisted a child's wrist in an effort to compel her to turn over a $20 bill she found on the floor (*Bisignano v. Harrison Central School District*, 2000). Further, educators can use reasonable force to defend themselves and others from harm.

DUE PROCESS

As indicated, since courts typically defer to educators who use reasonable forms of discipline in schools, the outcomes of student challenges often focus on whether the students received adequate procedural due process. As discussed with respect to *Goss v. Lopez* (1975) in greater detail below, the amount of procedural due process that students are entitled to depends on the seriousness of their offenses. In the most serious circumstances, as reflected in the IDEA, students who are subject to significant penalties such as expulsions and long-term suspensions (in excess of 10 days) are

> ...the amount of procedural due process that students are entitled to depends on the seriousness of their offenses.

entitled to notice and opportunities to respond in the presence of fair and impartial third-party decision makers (*In re Z. K.*, 2005).

Goss v. Lopez (*Goss*, 1975), wherein the Supreme Court established guide-lines for situations where students are subject to suspensions of 10 days or less, is arguably the high-water mark of students' rights. In *Goss*, students in Ohio challenged their 10-day suspensions for allegedly disruptive conduct on the basis that they were deprived of adequate procedural due process.

A careful reading of *Goss* reveals that the Supreme Court addressed the rules for two different types of student punishments and left the door open to a third, dealing with long-term suspensions and expulsions. The first, or lowest, level of procedural due process at issue in *Goss* concerned situa-tions when school rules are clearly defined in order to allow educators to maintain safe and orderly learning environments. As long as rules are rationally related to legitimate educational goals, such as maintaining safe and orderly learning environments, courts ordinarily enter judgments in favor of school officials. Among these types of rules that school officials may enforce at this level are such traditional items as not permitting stu-dents to talk or eat in class, prohibiting cheating on tests or running in halls, and forbidding fighting. The court continued to reiterate that as long as students knew or should have known the rules, and punishments were proportionate to their offenses, then educators could act almost summar-ily, since students have no right to procedural due process.

At its heart, *Goss* dealt with short-term student suspensions of 10 days or less. In deciding the case without addressing specific concerns, the Supreme Court recognized that, given the growth in size and complexity of schools over the past 30 years, directing educational officials to conduct too many hearings for students who were about to be subject to short-term suspensions could have been disruptive to the learning environment. The court feared that requiring hearings for relatively minor disciplinary infractions might have diverted school officials from more pressing con-cerns. To this end, the Court reasoned that

> some modicum of discipline and order is essential if the educa-tional function is to be performed. Events calling for discipline are frequent occurrences and sometimes require immediate, effective action. Suspension is considered not only to be a necessary tool to maintain order but a valuable educational device. The prospect of imposing elaborate hearing requirements in every suspension case is viewed with great concern. . . . (p. 580)

Ruling in favor of the students, the Court explained that while school officials must provide students with due process, there need be no delay between the time "notice" is given and the time of the hearing. In the great majority of cases the disciplinarian may informally discuss the alleged misconduct with the student minutes after it has occurred. We hold only that, in being given an opportunity to explain his version of the facts at this discussion, the student first be told what he is accused of doing and what the basis of the accusation is. (p. 582)

At the same time, the Court thought that if the presence of students constitutes threats of disruption, they may be removed immediately, and the due process requirements may be fulfilled as soon as is practicable. The Court expressly rejected the notion that students should be represented by counsel, be able to present witnesses, and be able to confront and cross-examine adverse witnesses in short-term exclusions from school.

Turning to the third level of student offenses, a question that was not at issue in *Goss,* the Court made it clear that "longer suspensions or expulsions for the remainder of the school term, or permanently, may require more formal procedures . . . [and that] in unusual situations, although involving only a short suspension, something more than the rudimentary procedures will be required" (p. 584). In light of the Court's suggestion, and as discussed in the next section, states have developed statutory guidelines addressing expulsions and long-term suspensions of students. Still, other than requiring fundamental fairness, courts and states do not agree on the exact nature of procedural due process in these situations.

Due Process Hearings

Before students may be subjected to long-term suspensions or expulsions, they are entitled to procedural due process. Yet, it is important to note that a so-called *Goss* hearing, as these disciplinary proceedings are sometimes called, are different from the due process hearings that are used when dealing with disputes involving the placement or discipline of students with disabilities. While both kinds of proceedings are administrative in nature, meaning that the rules of judicial evidence are greatly relaxed, they differ significantly.

> Before students may be subjected to long-term suspensions or expulsions, they are entitled to procedural due process.

On the one hand, due process hearings for students in special education placements are designed for decision makers to learn all of the facts in specific situations. On the other hand, *Goss* hearings are designed to ensure safe and orderly learning environments even as decision makers sift through evidence to determine whether students committed offenses worthy of major school sanctions. Further, although courts do not expect students to receive full judicial proceedings, students facing expulsions are entitled to notice informing them of the time and place of some form of hearings (*Donovan v. Ritchie*, 1995) as well as information about the charges they face (*C. B. by and through Breeding v. Driscoll*, 1996).

At a bare minimum, in addition to notice, student discipline must be resolved by fair and impartial third-party decision makers who base their actions on the contents of the records (*Newsome v. Batavia Local School District*, 1988). Some courts agree that students are not entitled to have attorneys present as trial counsel (*Newsome v. Batavia Local School District*, 1988; *Osteen v. Henley*, 1993), to know the identity of witnesses (*Brewer v. Austin Independent School District*, 1985; *Paredes by Koppenhoefer v. Curtis*, 1988), or to confront witnesses (*Newsome v. Batavia Local School District*, 1988; *Paredes by Koppenhoefer v. Curtis*, 1988), especially where there may be clear and serious danger to student witnesses (*Dillon v. Pulaski County Special School District*, 1978; *John A. v. San Bernardino City Unified School District*, 1982). Other courts are of the opinion that students lack a right to hearing officers who are not school employees (*John A. v. San Bernardino City Unified School District*, 1982) or to *Miranda* warnings against self-incrimination from educators (*In re L. A.*, 2001), school resource officers (*State v. J. H.*, 2005), or law enforcement officers who are assigned to schools on a regular basis and assigned duties beyond those of ordinary officers (*R. D. S. v. State*, 2008), when subjected to questioning by school officials.

In a controversy from Arkansas, the Eighth Circuit affirmed that a student failed to prove that school officials violated his procedural due process rights when he was expelled due to an altercation with a teacher and principal (*London v. Directors of DeWitt Public School*, 1999). The court agreed that educators did not violate the student's rights because they fully informed his mother why he was being expelled, and he received a hearing at which he was represented by counsel who had a full opportunity to question and cross-examine witnesses. The court added that although the educators broke board rules by not giving the student's attorney copies of the statements of two witnesses in advance of the hearing, this did not violate his constitutional rights.

On the other hand, some courts agreed that students do have a right to have an attorney present (*Givens v. Poe*, 1972; *Gonzales v. McEuen*, 1977), to cross-examine witnesses (*Colquitt v. Rich Township High School District No. 227*, 1998), to the presence of an impartial, nonschool, third-party decision maker (*Gonzales v. McEuen*, 1977), and to obtain an edited version of disciplinary records (*Graham v. West Babylon Union Free School District*, 1999).

In a related concern that highlights another difference between *Goss* hearings and due process hearings for students in special education, a state court in Illinois agreed with an almost 30-year-old federal case from Illinois (*Whitfield v. Simpson*, 1970) and a similar judgment from Massachusetts (*Pierce v. School Committee of New Bedford*, 1971) that students facing expulsions or long-term suspensions did not have a right to stenographic or mechanical recordings of proceedings. Conversely, more recently the highest court of Massachusetts maintained that officials had to grant a student's request for an electronic copy of testimony from a closed hearing (*Nicholas B. v. School Committee of Worcester*, 1992).

THE FOURTH AMENDMENT RIGHTS OF STUDENTS

It should not be surprising that the spread of violence in society as a whole made its presence known in schools. Societal increases in violence, coupled with the presence of contraband such as weapons and drugs, have led to a significant number of legal conflicts over the extent to which educators may search students and their property in attempts to maintain safe and orderly learning environments. This concern is reflected in a change in the IDEA, which now allows educators to transfer special education students to alternative educational settings for up to 45 school days as long as they impose similar penalties on students who are not disabled and the educators can determine that the students knowingly possessed, used, sold, or solicited drugs in schools or inflicted seriously bodily injury (20 U.S.C. § 1415(k)(1)(G)(ii); 34 C.F.R. § 300.530(g)(2)). The 45-day rule is discussed in further detail later in this book. Perhaps this modification was instituted in light of anecdotal reports that students who deal in or use drugs often ask children with disabilities, with whom they would not otherwise associate, to unknowingly transport their caches of drugs as a sign of friendship or as a favor.

> Societal increases in violence, coupled with the presence of contraband such as weapons and drugs, have led to a significant number of legal conflicts over the extent to which educators may search students and their property in attempts to maintain safe and orderly learning environments.

Searches of Students and Their Property

In relevant part, the Fourth Amendment to the U.S. Constitution reads: "The right of the people to be secure in their persons, houses, papers, and effects, against unreasonable searches and seizures, shall not be violated. . . ." Both this clause and the next, addressing search warrants, were long involved in criminal cases but had little impact in schools until the

1970s and did not play much of a role in educational settings until the Supreme Court's 1985 ruling in *New Jersey v. T. L. O.* In fact, since 1985, federal and state courts have addressed more than 300 cases on issues arising under the Fourth Amendment, whether dealing with searches of students and their persons or with drug testing (Russo & Mawdsley, 2008).

Beginning with the Supreme Court of California (*People v. Lanthier*, 1971), lower courts addressed the first round of cases involving the Fourth Amendment starting in 1971. That court allowed a locker search based on the smell that one emitted (*People v. Lanthier*, 1971), but later cases in the decade invalidated strip searches in schools for missing objects (*Bellnier v. Lund*, 1977; *Potts v. Wright*, 1973). Other courts reached mixed results on searches involving the use of sniff dogs. The Tenth Circuit (*Zamora v. Pomeroy*, 1981) and a federal trial court in Indiana (*Doe v. Renfrow*, 1979, 1980, 1981) upheld their use, while a federal trial court in Texas disagreed (*Jones v. Latexo Independent School District*, 1980). Moreover, the Fifth Circuit permitted the use of dogs to search students' cars but not their persons (*Horton v. Goose Creek Independent School District*, 1982, 1983).

The first, and only, case involving the search of a student in school to reach the Supreme Court is *New Jersey v. T. L. O.* (*T. L. O.*, 1985). The facts in *T. L. O.* are straightforward. A first-year high school student, identified in court documents as T. L. O. (because she was entitled to confidentiality insofar as the case was originally a juvenile delinquency proceeding), and a friend were accused of violating school rules by smoking cigarettes in a school lavatory. When confronted, the friend admitted to smoking and consequently was not brought to the office for a search. Insofar as T. L. O. not only denied that she was smoking but also claimed that she did not smoke at all, the teacher who suspected the girls of smoking brought her to the office of the assistant principal (AP). The AP then opened T. L. O.'s purse, without her permission, and saw her cigarettes "in plain view," a term of art borrowed from criminal law, which means that since he saw what he was looking for without going any further, the search was justified. On seeing them, the AP removed the cigarettes and accused T. L. O. of lying. When the AP proceeded with the search, he discovered

> a small amount of marihuana [*sic*], a pipe, a number of empty plastic bags, a substantial quantity of money in one-dollar bills, an index card that appeared to be a list of students who owed T. L. O. money, and two letters that implicated T. L. O. in marihuana [*sic*] dealing. (p. 328)

As a result of her confessing to selling marijuana at her high school, T. L. O. was adjudicated delinquent and sentenced to a year on probation.

"First, one must consider 'whether the . . . action was justified at its inception'; second, one must determine whether the search as actually conducted 'was reasonably related in scope to the circumstances which justified the interference in the first place'" (*T. L. O.*, 1985, p. 341).

Yet, an intermediate appellate court and the New Jersey Supreme Court agreed that since the search of T. L. O.'s purse violated her Fourth Amendment rights, the adjudication had to be dismissed. When the State of New Jersey sought further review, something that it could do because the case involved a juvenile delinquency proceeding, not a criminal conviction, the U.S. Supreme Court reversed in its favor. Although the Court ruled that the Fourth Amendment's prohibition against unreasonable searches and seizures applies in public schools, the Court went on to craft a two-part test to measure the legality of school searches.

According to the Supreme Court, when reviewing student searches in school settings,

> first, one must consider "whether the . . . action was justified at its inception"; second, one must determine whether the search as actually conducted "was reasonably related in scope to the circumstances which justified the interference in the first place." (*T. L. O.*, 1985, p. 341)

Second, the Court held that

> a search will be permissible in its scope when the measures adopted are reasonably related to the objectives of the search and not excessively intrusive in light of the age and sex of the student and the nature of the infraction. (*T. L. O.*, 1985, p. 342)

"A search will be permissible in its scope when the measures adopted are reasonably related to the objectives of the search and not excessively intrusive in light of the age and sex of the student and the nature of the infraction" (*T. L. O.*, 1985, p. 342).

As to the first part of the test, the Court specified that a search is justified at its inception "when there are reasonable grounds for suspecting that the search will turn up evidence that the student has violated or is violating either the law or the rules of the school" (*T. L. O.*, 1985, p. 342). Reasonable suspicion, which is a subjective measure, must be based on specific facts that are more than a hunch. Unlike the much higher standard of probable cause, which applies to the police, reasonable suspicion requires only some articulable justification in order for school officials to conduct searches. To the extent that so-called administrative, or school, searches are designed to ensure student safety rather than gather evidence for criminal

prosecutions, courts typically allow school officials to conduct searches under the lower reasonable suspicion standard.

Turning to the second part of the test, when
considering the totality of circumstances, courts
acknowledge that educators may have to count on
the dependability of witnesses in considering
whether to search students or their property. As
noted in the test, when evaluating whether there

> A search is justified at its
> inception "when there are
> reasonable grounds for suspecting
> that the search will turn up
> evidence that the student has
> violated or is violating either the
> law or the rules of the school"
> (*T. L. O.,* 1985, p. 342).

was justification to proceed with a search, courts consider such elements as
the source(s) of information, a student's record, the seriousness and preva-
lence of a problem, and the urgency of making a search. Put another way, the
more serious the offense and the greater the need to protect students and others in school communities, then the greater the justification for educators to
carry out searches.

Courts have upheld searches based on information supplied by
students (*Commonwealth v. Snyder,* 1992; *Wofford v. Evans,* 2004), parents
(*United States v. Aguilera,* 2003), school employees (*Cornfield by Lewis v.
Consolidated High School District No. 230,* 1993), and the police (*In re D. E. M.,*
1999). Moreover, when school security officers operating in schools function as educators rather than traditional police officers, a growing number
of courts agree that they are subject to the reasonable suspicion standard
(*People v. Dilworth,* 1996; *R. B. v. State,* 2008; *R. D. S. v. State,* 2008) rather
than probable cause (*State v. K. L. M.,* 2006) because their primary concern
is student safety rather than criminal investigations. However, when
searches are based on anonymous tips, most (*In re Cody S.,* 2004; *State v.
Bullard,* 2005), but not all (*In re Doe,* 2004; *People v. Kline,* 2005), courts
agreed that they are acceptable if the situation meets other requirements
for acceptability, such as the urgency of the need for a search.

Recognizing that different types of searches involve varying levels of
intrusiveness, courts have generally sustained searches of students' cars
(*Anders ex rel. Anders v. Fort Wayne Community Schools,* 2000; *Covington
County v. G. W.,* 2000), lockers (*In re Isiah B.,* 1993a, 1993b; *Zamora v.
Pomeroy,* 1981) (in which students already have a greatly diminished
expectation of privacy, since lockers are school property), and backpacks
(*In re F. B.,* 1999a, 1999b; *In re Murray,* 2000) for routine administrative purposes connected with the general welfare of the schools, even if the stu-
dents are off campus, as long as officials have reasonable suspicion that
students violated either school rules (*Rhodes v. Guarricino,* 1999) or the law
(*Commonwealth v. Williams,* 2000).

At the same time, courts generally uphold searches by metal detectors (*In
re F. B.,* 1999a, 1999b; *Thompson v. Carthage School District,* 1996), including

hand-held devices that are used in individual searches (*State v. J. A.*, 1996, 1997a, 1997b), because they are highly reliable and minimally intrusive. Additionally, courts generally allow the use of sniff dogs (*Bundick v. Bay City Independent School District*, 2001; *Commonwealth v. Cass*, 1998a, 1998b; *Marner v. Eufaula City School Board*, 2002) unless they get too close to children. In one such case, the Ninth Circuit rejected the use of a sniff dog on the basis that stationing a dog at classroom doors in California, in close proximity to students, was unreasonable, because doing so violated the children's rights to privacy (*B. C. v. Plumas Unified School District*, 1999).

Courts have reached mixed results with regard to the most intrusive form of searches, strip searches. The majority (see, e.g., *Kennedy v. Dexter Consolidated Schools*, 2000; *State ex rel. Galford v. Mark Anthony B.*, 1993; *Thomas ex rel. Thomas v. Roberts*, 2001) but not all (*Cornfield by Lewis v. Consolidated High School District No. 230*, 1993; *Jenkins v. Talladega City Board of Education*, 1997a, 1997b; *Williams ex rel. Williams v. Ellington*, 1991) cases have struck down strip searches for personal items rather than drugs or other forms of contraband. In a related concern, again, most (see, e.g., *Jenkins v. Talladega City Board of Education*, 1997a, 1997b; *Williams ex rel. Williams v. Ellington*, 1991), but not all (*Bell v. Marseilles Elementary School*, 2001; *Fewless v. Board of Education*, 2002), courts refused to impose personal liability on educators for unreasonable strip searches, since case law did not clearly establish that their actions were unconstitutional under the circumstances.

In a situation involving one of the most intrusive searches, the Seventh Circuit upheld a strip search of a student in Illinois that occurred in 1991 (*Cornfield by Lewis v. Consolidated High School District No. 230*, *Cornfield*, 1993). A teacher and an AP searched the student for drugs even though his mother refused to consent to a pat down, and he became visibly agitated when officials told him that he was going to be searched. During the search, two educators had the student disrobe in their presence and visually inspected his naked body and examined his clothes but could not find any drugs. Even so, the court affirmed that since there was reasonable suspicion, school officials met both prongs of the *T. L. O.* test.

Perhaps the most interesting aspect of *Cornfield* for the purpose of this book is that the court failed to give much weight to the student's having been enrolled in a behavior disorder program at his high school other than making two brief acknowledgments of his condition. The court commented on the student's placement in its opening statement and later wrote that "the fact that students in such a program exhibit inconsistent behavior and that drug users behave erratically does not lead inevitably to a conclusion that a student in a behavioral disorder program is a drug user" (p. 1322). While it may be difficult to argue with the court's logic in the end, it is worth keeping in mind that at that time the IDEA lacked clear standards on discipline and also failed to address whether behavior that was otherwise subject to discipline would be subject to a manifestation determination or a behavioral intervention plan for special education students.

DRUG TESTING

Just as problems were emerging in schools with regard to violence and weapons, so, too, did the increase in drug use in society as a whole impact on students in elementary, and mostly secondary, education (Russo & Gregory, 1999). The first case involving drugs in schools arose in Indiana when, in response to having baseball players test positive for marijuana, their school board implemented a random drug testing policy for student-athletes and cheerleaders. Three years after *T. L. O.,* the Seventh Circuit affirmed that drug testing passed constitutional muster under the Fourth Amendment, since educational officials in Indiana built in adequate safeguards to protect student privacy (*Schaill v. Tippecanoe County School Corp.,* 1988).

The Supreme Court first entered the fray over suspicionless drug testing of student-athletes in a dispute from Oregon, *Vernonia School District 47J v. Acton* (*Acton,* 1995). Insofar as parents were concerned that their sons, student-athletes, were involved in drug use, they petitioned their school board for help. In response, the board implemented a drug testing policy for student-athletes on the grounds that student-athletes were leaders of the school's drug culture. In addition, the facts revealed that on at least two occasions, student-athletes were injured due to the effects of drugs. Students who wished to participate in interscholastic sports were required to submit to a urinalysis drug test. The policy, which was primarily rehabilitative, rather than punitive, in nature, included extensive safeguards with regard to the collection of urine samples that were designed to protect the privacy rights of the student-athletes.

Acton began when a seventh-grade student and his parents challenged his being denied the opportunity to play interscholastic football after they refused to sign a form consenting to drug testing. The student and his parents claimed that the policy violated the Fourth Amendment and the state constitution, since there was no evidence that he used drugs. After a federal trial court upheld the policy, the Ninth Circuit struck it down as unconstitutional. On further review in *Acton* (1995), the Supreme Court vacated and remanded in favor of the board.

In *Acton,* the Supreme Court applied a three-part test upholding the policy's constitutionality. Insofar as the Court applied essentially the same test seven years later in *Board of Education of Independent School District No. 92 of Pottawatomie v. Earls* (*Earls,* 2002a), the test is identified here but discussed below. First, the Court considered the nature of the privacy issue involved, asserting that students have a lesser expectation of privacy than ordinary cit-izens. Second, the Court considered the character of the intrusion and was satisfied that the search was constitutional, because urinalysis testing was minimally intrusive in light of the safeguards that the board instituted. Third, the Court considered the nature and immediacy of the board's con-cern and the efficacy of testing in meeting its goal, concluding that the board articulated an acceptable reason for suspicionless drug testing.

As with so many emerging legal issues, *Acton* failed to resolve all issues as lower federal courts remained split over suspicionless testing of students involved in extracurricular activities. For instance, in another case from Indiana, the Seventh Circuit, relying on precedent due to its con-cerns about testing, twice upheld suspicionless drug testing for student-athletes (*Joy v. Penn-Harris-Madison School Corp.*, 2000; *Todd v. Rush County Schools*, 1998a, 1998b) but struck down mandatory drug and alcohol test-ing of students who were suspended for three or more days for fighting (*Willis v. Anderson Community School Corp.*, 1998). The court observed that absent a relationship between students' misbehavior and drug or alcohol use, testing was impermissible. Further, in a case from Oklahoma that made its way to the Supreme Court, the Tenth Circuit struck down ran-dom drug testing as unconstitutional (*Earls ex rel. Earls v. Board of Education of Tecumseh Public School District*, 2001). Moreover, in a case not involving a student-athlete, the Third Circuit affirmed that school officials did not vio-late the constitution when, consistent with board policy, officials subjected a student who was suspected of being on drugs to urinalysis testing (*Hedges v. Musco*, 2000).

Earls began when a school board in Oklahoma enacted a student activi-ties drug testing policy that required all middle and high school students to submit to urinalysis testing for drugs in order to participate in extracurricu-lar activities. Ultimately, the policy was limited to participants in extracur-ricular activities that were sanctioned by the state's secondary schools activities association. As in *Acton*, students and their parents filed suit, pri-marily alleging that the policy violated the Fourth Amendment absent a need to test participants due to the presence of a drug problem at school.

Relying on *Acton*, a federal trial court granted the board's motion for summary judgment, but the Tenth Circuit reversed in favor of the stu-dents. The Supreme Court, in *Board of Education of Independent School District No. 92 of Pottawatomie v. Earls* (*Earls*, 2002a), in turn, reversed in favor of the board. Prior to applying *Acton*, the Supreme Court reiterated that whether to permit drug testing requires a fact-specific balancing of the Fourth Amendment

The Supreme Court began by remarking that "we first consider the nature of the privacy interest allegedly compromised by the drug testing" (*Earls*, 2002a, p. 830).

rights of students against a school board's legitimate interests to avoid a problem with drugs in school. The Court thus applied the three-part test that it created in *Acton*.

In applying its tripartite analysis of the board policy, the Supreme Court began by remarking that "we first consider the nature of the privacy interest allegedly compromised by the drug testing" (*Earls*, 2002a, p. 830). The Court ruled that the combination of students' limited privacy interests—based on the fact that they voluntarily subject themselves to great intrusions on their privacy through such activities as common locker rooms—coupled with educators' need to maintain safety and discipline meant that the policy passed constitutional muster.

Next, the Court turned to "consider the character of the intrusion imposed by the policy" (*Earls*, 2002a, p. 832) in light of the safeguards that the policy included to protect student privacy, such as having females produce urine samples in closed bathroom stalls, having the results being kept confidential and shared on a need-to-know basis with a limited number of school officials, and refusing to share the results of positive tests with enforcement officials. Moreover, since school officials used the test results only to impose sanctions on students with respect to their ability to participate in extracurricular activities, the Court found that the policy was constitutional.

> Next, the Court turned to "consider the character of the intrusion imposed by the policy" (*Earls*, 2002a, p. 832).

Finally, the Supreme Court turned to "consider the nature and immediacy of the government's concerns and the efficacy of the Policy in meeting them" (*Earls*, 2002a, p. 834). Unlike *Acton*, where drugs were already a problem, the Court agreed with school officials that they were free to adopt a proactive stance to prevent drug problems from occurring rather than wait until there was an actual problem before permitting educators to implement a policy of suspicionless testing. Accordingly, the Court decreed that the policy was constitutional.

> Finally, the Supreme Court turned to "consider the nature and immediacy of the government's concerns and the efficacy of the Policy in meeting them" (*Earls*, 2002a, p. 834).

Following *Earls*, disputes continued to emerge over the appropriateness of suspicionless drug testing. For example, a federal trial court in Pennsylvania upheld drug testing of a student-athlete in light of his coach's fears that his continuing to use drugs had the potential to harm the student (*Dominic J. v. Wyoming Valley West High School*, 2005). Further, the Indiana Supreme Court upheld random testing for use of alcohol and drugs but not for use of tobacco products by students who participated in athletic, extracurricular, or cocurricular activities as well as by those who wished to drive to and from school (*Linke v. Northwestern School Corp.*, 2002). (As to the novel item of tobacco, the court decided that educators could not subject students to nicotine testing due to their negligible interest in this regard.) However, a federal trial court in Texas struck down as unreasonable a drug testing policy that would have applied to all students in junior and senior high school for the duration of the academic year (*Tannahill ex rel. Tannahill v. Lockney Independent School District*, 2001). The court found that the policy was unconstitutional not only because the board lacked a compelling interest to test students but also because drug use in the school was actually lower than in other schools.

In an aspect of drug testing that may be crucial when dealing with students with disabilities who have individualized education programs (IEPs), it is important to keep in mind that many of them may take prescription medications to help them make it through the school day. As such, it is important to recall that the recent amendments to the IDEA prohibit school officials from requiring parents to obtain prescriptions for their children for psychotropic substances such as Ritalin that are covered by the Controlled Substances Act as a condition of attending school, being evaluated, or receiving special education services (20 U.S.C. § 1412(a)(25)). In light of this change, educators should be careful to avoid even suggesting to parents that their children with disabilities should be medicated if they wish to attend school. Even so, educators would be wise to keep in mind that since some special education students do take prescription medications that may well impact the outcome of drug testing, they would be prudent to require students who are on IEPs, and their parents, to provide a list of prescription drugs that they are taking so as to avoid unnecessary complications with the outcome of testing.

Some frequently asked questions about due process, searches, and drug testing are summarized in Figure 2.1.

SUMMARY

Discipline is perhaps the most challenging duty that educators must carry out on a daily basis, and the task is complicated by the special rules for disciplining students with disabilities that are discussed in the rest of this book. As school officials seek to balance the potentially conflicting interests that arise between their duty to impose reasonable discipline in order to maintain safe and orderly learning environments and their duty to safeguard student rights, they would be wise to keep due process and equal protection, as discussed earlier in this book, in mind when disciplining students and when considering actions covered by the Fourth Amendment.

Figure 2.1   Frequently Asked Questions

Q. What due process is required before a student can be given a short-term suspension?

A. In *Goss v. Lopez* (1975), the U.S. Supreme Court declared that students may be suspended or expelled from school as long as they are given certain due process safeguards. At a minimum, suspensions of 10 days or fewer require informal notice of the charges and the opportunity for some sort of hearing. If the students deny the charges, they must be told of the evidence and given the opportunity for rebuttal. These standards are flexible, depending on the nature and severity of the misconduct and the intended punishment. The hearing may take place immediately and may involve no more than the normal questioning of a student by an administrator. As long as the students have been informed of the charges and the evidence against them, and have been given the opportunity to respond, the elements of due process have been met.

Q. What additional due process requirements exist when students face more serious consequences such as expulsion?

A. Stricter adherence to due process is required for more severe infractions and penalties. Suspensions of more than 10 days, or expulsions, require additional due process. Although the Supreme Court in *Goss* did not outline the requirements of due process for students facing expulsions, due to the seriousness of the consequence, they should be given a quasi-judicial hearing that would include the right to be represented by counsel and the opportunity to present and cross-examine witnesses. Due process requirements for students facing expulsions may be spelled out in state law.

Q. May school officials search the lockers, backpacks, and purses of students with disabilities?

A. To the extent that school officials act based on reasonable suspicion or according to articulated plans on suspicionless searches, educators are free to search students with disabilities in the same way they search other students, since all students have diminished expectations of privacy in school. Of course, if officials discover contraband such as drugs or weapons, then the IDEA's 45-day rule may come into play such that students can be placed in alternative interim placements while officials and parents seek to develop more appropriate placements.

Q. May school officials submit students with disabilities who participate in extracurricular activities to drug testing?

A. Again, to the extent that school officials act based on reasonable suspicion or according to articulated plans on suspicionless searches, educators are free to treat students with disabilities who participate in extracurricular activities in the same way as they treat other students. However, since many students with disabilities who participate in extracurricular activities may take prescription medications, educators would be wise to keep an updated list of the legal drugs that students take so as to avoid any unnecessary conflicts should they be tested and yield positive results.

RECOMMENDATIONS FOR PRACTITIONERS

- Educators at the building level should annually review, and revise, their policies as reflected in student discipline handbooks, making sure that the building policies are consistent with board policies as well as with applicable state and federal laws.

- Policies should

  1. specify what rules apply to special education students whose misbehaviors are not manifestations of their disabilities; of course, this part of policies/handbooks must refer to and be consistent with the law relating to manifestation determination.

  2. provide students who are subject to discipline with substantive and procedural due process.

- With respect to specific types of punishments, policies should

  1. clarify the boundaries of the kinds of verbal punishments that teachers may use.

  2. explain when students may be sent to time-out rooms and for how long they may/must remain in such locations.

  3. specify, in states that allow corporal punishment, the circumstances under which it can be imposed, whether parents or students' IEPs must address its use for minor infractions, by whom it can be imposed, whether any witnesses must be present, whether it is limited to students' buttocks, whether parents must give permission in advance, and whether reaching a set number of instances of corporal punishment (such as three in a school year) might require parental conferences.

- When dealing with suspensions and expulsions, again ensure that these punishments are imposed in accord with students' IEPs and are imposed after any necessary manifestation determinations.

  1. Policies for short-term suspensions (less than 10 days) should address an exemplary list of items that can lead to such exclusions along with such specific items as whether students may

     a) serve their punishments in school.
     b) be allowed to make up work that they miss.
     c) appeal suspensions, and if so, to whom appeals go and time lines for resolution of appeals.

  2. Policies for long-term suspensions (in excess of 10 days) should provide an exemplary list of items that can lead to such exclusions along with such specific items as

a) how soon after infractions students and their parents must be notified of the charges that they face.

b) how students are to be informed of the evidence against them.

c) when and where due process hearings are to occur.

d) how the school will ensure that due process hearings are conducted by fair and impartial third-party decisions makers.

e) appeals procedures.

- When dealing with searches and seizures, policies should begin with clear statements that since school boards own their lockers, students have diminished expectations of privacy. Policies should also include clear guidelines addressing such matters as

1. what areas may be searched.

2. when searches may occur.

3. who may conduct searches.

4. whether searches are to be videotaped for evidentiary purposes.

5. the circumstances under which police may be involved.

- When dealing with drug testing, a policy should

1. explain whether it will be employed generally or is limited to students who are involved in extracurricular activities.

2. identify the circumstances under which it will be used, such as whether tests will be suspicion based or whether random suspicionless testing will be conducted.

3. include statements indicating that rehabilitation and counseling is the primary goal rather than punishment.

4. (consistent with the policies in *Acton* and *Earls*) address such practical items as

   a) who pays for testing.

   b) what drugs are being tested for.

   c) what kind of samples are to be collected, such as urine, saliva, or hair.

   d) who supervises the collection of samples.

   e) a clear chain of possession of samples.

   f) who tests samples.

   g) whether samples are used in their entirety or split and retested in the event of positive results.

   h) who is notified of tests.

   i) time frames within which notification occurs.

   j) whether students have the right to rely on the results of tests that they had conducted independently.

      k) whether students may challenge positive results consistent with the due process procedures identified above.

- As with notice requirements, when dealing with students with disabilities, educational leaders should require parents and qualified students, regardless of whether they are in regular or special education, to sign and return forms that acknowledge that they have read, understand, and intend to abide by the rules established in student handbooks.

WHAT'S NEXT

The remainder of this book is concerned with the application of disciplinary policies and procedures to students with disabilities. Inasmuch as these students have additional rights created by the IDEA, disciplinary procedures need to be adjusted when the consequence may affect the students' fundamental rights to a free appropriate public education. The next chapter reviews the procedures established by the IDEA and other laws protecting the rights of students with disabilities. It includes an historical review of case law that led to the implementation of the IDEA's current disciplinary provisions.

REFERENCES

Anders ex rel. Anders v. Fort Wayne Community Schools, 124 F. Supp.2d 618 (N.D. Ind. 2000).

B. C. v. Plumas Unified School District, 192 F.3d 1260 (9th Cir. 1999).

Baker v. Owen, 395 F. Supp. 294 (M.D. N.C. 1975a), *affirmed,* 423 U.S. 907 (1975b).

Bell v. Marseilles Elementary School, 160 F. Supp.2d 883 (N.D. Ill. 2001).

Bellnier v. Lund, 438 F. Supp. 47 (N.D. N.Y. 1977).

Bisignano v. Harrison Central School District, 113 F. Supp.2d 591 (S.D. N.Y. 2000).

Board of Education of Independent School District No. 92 of Pottawatomie v. Earls, 536 U.S. 822 (2002a), *on remand,* 300 F.3d 1222 (10th Cir. 2002b).

Brewer v. Austin Independent School District, 779 F.2d 260 (5th Cir. 1985).

Brown ex rel. Brown v. Ramsey, 121 F. Supp.2d 911 (E.D. Va. 2000).

Bundick v. Bay City Independent School District, 140 F. Supp.2d 735 (S.D. Tex. 2001).

Bunger v. Iowa High School Athletic Association, 197 N.W.2d 555 (Iowa 1972).

C. B. by and through Breeding v. Driscoll, 82 F.3d 383 (11th Cir. 1996).

C. R. K., In re, 56 S.W.3d 288 (Tex. Ct. App. 2001).

Code of Federal Regulations (C.F.R.), as cited.

Cody S., In re, 16 Cal. Rptr.3d 653 (Cal. Ct. App. 2004).

Cole by Cole v. Greenfield–Central Community Schools, 657 F. Supp. 56 (S.D. Ind. 1986).

Colquitt v. Rich Township High School District No. 227, 699 N.E.2d 1109 (Ill. App. Ct. 1998).

Commonwealth v. Cass, 709 A.2d 350 (Pa. 1998a), *cert. denied*, 525 U.S. 833 (1998b).

Commonwealth v. Snyder, 597 N.E.2d 1363 (Mass. 1992).

Commonwealth v. Williams, 749 A.2d 957 (Pa. Commw. Ct. 2000).

Cornfield by Lewis v. Consolidated High School District No. 230, 991 F.2d 1316 (7th Cir. 1993).

Costello v. Mitchell Public School District 79, 266 F.3d 916 (8th Cir. 2001).

Covington County v. G. W., 767 So. 2d 187 (Miss. 2000).

D. A. D., In Interest of, 481 S.E.2d 262 (Ga. Ct. App. 1997).

D. E. M., In re, 727 A.2d 570 (Pa. Super. Ct. 1999).

Dillon v. Pulaski County Special School District, 468 F. Supp. 54 (E.D. Ark. 1978).

Doe, In re, 91 P.3d 485 (Hawaii 2004).

Doe v. Renfrow, 475 F. Supp. 1012 (N.D. Ind. 1979), *reversed in part on other grounds*, 631 F.2d 91 (7th Cir. 1980) (*per curiam*), *cert. denied*, 451 U.S. 1022 (1981).

Dominic J. v. Wyoming Valley West High School, 362 F. Supp.2d 560 (M.D. Pa. 2005).

Donovan v. Ritchie, 68 F.3d 14 (1st Cir. 1995).

Earls ex rel. Earls v. Board of Education of Tecumseh Public School District, 242 F.3d 1264 (10th Cir. 2001), *cert. granted*, 534 U.S. 1015 (2001).

F. B., In re, 726 A.2d 361 (Pa. 1999a), *cert. denied sub nom. F. B. v. Pennsylvania*, 528 U.S. 1060 (1999b).

Fewless v. Board of Education, 208 F. Supp.2d 806 (W.D. Mich. 2002).

Fox v. Cleveland, 169 F. Supp.2d 977 (W.D. Ark. 2001).

Fuller ex rel. Fuller v. Decatur Public School Board of Education School District 61, 251 F.3d 662 (7th Cir. 2001).

Garcia v. Miera, 817 F.2d 650 (10th Cir. 1987), *cert. denied*, 485 U.S. 959 (1988).

Givens v. Poe, 346 F. Supp. 202 (W.D. N.C. 1972).

Gonzales v. McEuen, 435 F. Supp. 460 (C.D. Cal. 1977).

Goss v. Lopez, 419 U.S. 565 (1975).

Gottlieb ex rel. Calabria v. Laurel Highlands School District, 272 F.3d 168 (3d Cir. 2001).

Graham v. West Babylon Union Free School District, 692 N.Y.S.2d 460 (N.Y. App. Div. 1999).

Hall v. Tawney, 621 F.2d 607 (4th Cir. 1980).

Hedges v. Musco, 204 F.3d 109 (3d Cir. 2000).

Honig v. Doe, 484 U.S. 305 (1988).

Horton v. Goose Creek Independent School District, 690 F.2d 470 (5th Cir. 1982), *cert. denied*, 463 U.S. 1207 (1983).

Individuals with Disabilities Education Act (IDEA), 20 U.S.C. § 1400–1482 (2006).

Ingraham v. Wright, 430 U.S. 651 (1977).

Isiah B., In re, 500 N.W.2d 637 (Wis. 1993a), *cert. denied*, 510 U.S. 884 (1993b).

J. H., In re, 797 A.2d 260 (Pa. Super. Ct. 2002).

Jenkins v. Talladega City Board of Education, 115 F.3d 821 (11th Cir. 1997a), *cert. denied, sub nom. Jenkins by Hall v. Herring*, 522 U.S. 966 (1997b).

John A. v. San Bernardino City Unified School District, 654 P.2d 242 (Cal. 1982).

Jones v. Latexo Independent School District, 499 F. Supp. 223 (E.D. Tex. 1980).

Joy v. Penn-Harris-Madison School Corp., 212 F.3d 1052 (7th Cir. 2000).

Kennedy v. Dexter Consolidated Schools, 10 P.3d 115 (N.M. 2000).

L. A., In re, 21 P.3d 952 (Kan. 2001).

Linke v. Northwestern School Corp., 763 N.E.2d 972 (Ind. 2002).

London v. Directors of DeWitt Public School, 194 F.3d 873 (8th Cir. 1999).

M. C. v. State, 695 So.2d 477 (Fla. Dist. Ct. App. 1997), *review denied*, 700 So.2d 686 (Fla. 1997).

Marner v. Eufaula City School Board, 204 F. Supp.2d 1318 (M.D. Ala. 2002).

Mazevski v. Horseheads Central School District, 950 F. Supp. 69 (W.D. N.Y. 1997).

Meeker v. Edmundson, 415 F.3d 317 (4th Cir. 2005).

Murray, In re, 525 S.E.2d 496 (N.C. Ct. App. 2000).

Neal v. Fulton County Board of Education, 229 F.3d 1069 (11th Cir. 2000), *rehearing en banc denied*, 244 F.3d 143 (11th Cir. 2000).

New Jersey v. T. L. O., 469 U.S. 325 (1985).

Newsome v. Batavia Local School District, 842 F.2d 920 (6th Cir. 1988).

Nicholas B. v. School Committee of Worcester, 587 N.E.2d 211 (Mass. 1992).

Osteen v. Henley, 13 F.3d 221 (7th Cir. 1993).

Paredes by Koppenhoefer v. Curtis, 864 F.2d 426 (6th Cir. 1988).

People v. Dilworth, 661 N.E.2d 310 (Ill. 1996), *cert. denied*, 517 U.S. 1197 (1996).

People v. Kline, 824 N.E.2d 295 (Ill. App. Ct. 2005), *appeal denied*, 833 N.E.2d 6 (Ill. 2005).

People v. Lanthier, 488 P.2d 625 (Cal. 1971).

Pierce v. School Committee of New Bedford, 322 F. Supp. 957 (D. Mass. 1971).

Potts v. Wright, 357 F. Supp. 215 (E.D. Pa. 1973).

R. B. v. State, 975 So. 2d 546 (Fla. Dist. Ct. App. 2008), *review denied*, 2008 WL 2634489 (Fla. 2008).

R. D. S. v. State, 245 S.W.3d 356 (Tenn. 2008).

Randall, D. (2008). *States with corporal punishment in school*. Retrieved July 31, 2008, from http://school.familyeducation.com/classroom-discipline/resource/38377.html

Rhodes v. Guarricino, 54 F. Supp.2d 186 (S.D. N.Y. 1999).

Russo, C. J., & Gregory, D. L. (1999). Legal and ethical issues surrounding drug testing in schools. *Law Review of Michigan State University Detroit College of Law*, 1999(3), 611–644.

Russo, C. J., & Mawdsley, R. D. (2008). *Searches, seizures and drug testing procedures: Balancing rights and school safety* (2nd ed.). Sarasota, FL: LRP.

S. M. ex rel. L. G. v. Lakeland School District, 33 Fed. Appx. 635 (3d Cir. 2002).

Schaill v. Tippecanoe County School Corp., 864 F.2d 1309 (7th Cir. 1988).

Schultzen v. Woodbury Central Community School District, 187 F. Supp.2d 1099 (N.D. Iowa 2002).

Smith ex rel. Smith v. Half Hollow Hills Central School District, 298 F.3d 168 (2d Cir. 2002).

State ex rel. Galford v. Mark Anthony B., 433 S.E.2d 41 (W. Va. 1993).

State v. Bullard, 891 So.2d 1158 (Fla. Dist. Ct. App. 2005).

State v. J. A., 679 So.2d 316 (Fla. Dist. Ct. App. 1996), *rehearing denied* (1996), *review denied*, 689 So.2d 1069 (Fla. 1997a), *cert. denied*, 522 U.S. 831 (1997b).

State v. J. H., 898 So.2d 240 (Fla. Dist. Ct. App. 2005).

State v. K. L. M., 628 S.E.2d 651 (Ga. Ct. App. 2006).

Tannahill ex rel. Tannahill v. Lockney Independent School District, 133 F. Supp.2d 919 (N.D. Tex. 2001).

Thomas ex rel. Thomas v. Roberts, 261 F.3d 1160 (11th Cir. 2001).

Thompson v. Carthage School District, 87 F.3d 979 (8th Cir. 1996).

Todd v. Rush County Schools, 133 F.3d 984 (7th Cir. 1998a), *cert. denied*, 525 U.S. 824 (1998b).

Trustees of Lincoln County School District No. 13, Eureka v. Holden, 754 P.2d 506 (Mont. 1988).

United States Code (U.S.C.), as cited.

United States v. Aguilera, 287 F. Supp.2d. 1204 (E.D. Cal. 2003).

Vernonia School District 47J v. Acton, 515 U.S. 646 (1995).

Wallace by Wallace v. Batavia School District 101, 68 F.3d 1010 (7th Cir. 1995).

Wexell v. Scott, 276 N.E.2d 735 (Ill. App. Ct. 1971).

Whitfield v. Simpson, 312 F. Supp. 889 (E.D. Ill. 1970).

Widdoes v. Detroit Public Schools, 619 N.W.2d 12 (Mich. Ct. App. 2000), *appeal denied*, 625 N.W.2d 785 (Mich. 2001).

Williams ex rel. Williams v. Ellington, 936 F.2d 881 (6th Cir. 1991).

Willis v. Anderson Community School Corp., 158 F.3d 415 (7th Cir. 1998).

Wofford v. Evans, 390 F.3d 318 (4th Cir. 2004).

Wood v. Strickland, 420 U.S. 308, 325 (1975), *rehearing denied*, 421 U.S. 921 (1975), *on remand sub nom. Strickland v. Inlow*, 519 F.2d 744 (8th Cir. 1975).

Z. K., *In re*, 695 N.W.2d 656 (Minn. Ct. App. 2005).

Zamora v. Pomeroy, 639 F.2d 662 (10th Cir. 1981).

Zellman ex rel. M. Z. v. Independent School District No. 2758, 594 N.W.2d 216 (Minn. Ct. App. 1999).

Zirkel, P. A. (2002). Discipline of students with disabilities. *Education Law Reporter, 174*, 43–54.

3 Laws Affecting Discipline for Students With Disabilities

Key Concepts in This Chapter

♦ The Individuals With Disabilities Education Act

♦ Section 504 of the Rehabilitation Act

♦ The Americans With Disabilities Act

♦ Early Case Law

♦ Amendments to the Individuals With Disabilities Education Act

INTRODUCTION

Students in American schools are not always as well behaved as educators and parents might like them to be. Consequently, school authorities must take disciplinary actions against misbehaving students from time to time. Most disciplinary actions result in a loss of privileges for students but do not result in losses of educational opportunities. Yet, sometimes more severe sanctions are imposed that do result in the losses of educational privileges. School officials have used suspensions and expulsions as disciplinary sanctions for many years.

As indicated in Chapter 2, suspensions are usually defined as short-term exclusions, while expulsions are long-term exclusions from school. From a legal perspective, suspensions of longer than 10 consecutive school days are treated much like expulsions, especially for students with disabilities. Students facing significant disciplinary actions are entitled to at least minimal due process before school officials may impose such penalties.

Students with disabilities who face disciplinary actions have rights that place additional due process requirements on school officials. Insofar as expulsions result in deprivations of educational opportunities and possibly infringements on rights guaranteed by the Individuals with Disabilities Education Act (IDEA, 2006) and other federal statutes, further due process safeguards must be put in place when dealing with students who are on individualized education programs (IEPs). In fact, the U.S. Supreme Court, in *Honig v. Doe* (*Honig*, 1988), suggested that the IDEA was passed, in part, to prevent school officials from impermissibly excluding students whose disabilities resulted in behavior problems.

The IDEA, as originally enacted, did not include language that specifically referenced discipline. In 1997 and again in 2004, Congress amended the IDEA to include specific procedural requirements for the disciplinary process. Prior to the

> The IDEA, as originally enacted, did not include language that specifically referenced discipline.

passage of the 1997 amendments, a significant body of case law developed that provided school boards and administrators (as well as their lawyers) with new requirements for disciplining students with disabilities. Most of the 1997 and 2004 IDEA disciplinary provisions evolved from that case law. As such, an analysis of the case law that existed before the 1997 amendments were enacted can provide much guidance on how the IDEA's current provisions should be implemented.

This chapter presents a general overview of the statutes that affect how school administrators may discipline students with disabilities. In view of the fact that many of the current disciplinary sections of the IDEA evolved from case law, the chapter also offers an historical perspective of the judicial decisions that led up to the inclusion of the discipline sections in the current version of the IDEA. An understanding of how the case law evolved and provided the basis for the statutory provisions is important to understanding how these mandates are to be implemented.

STATUTES RELEVANT TO STUDENTS WITH DISABILITIES

The IDEA is the major federal statute providing educational rights to students with disabilities. Even so, two other statutes, Section 504 of the Rehabilitation Act (Rehabilitation Act, Section 504, 2006) and the Americans with Disabilities Act, which was modified recently (ADA,

2006, 2008), also have implications for the disciplinary process when it involves students with disabilities (Russo & Osborne, 2009). These statutes are basically civil rights laws that prohibit discrimination against individuals who have impairments that substantially limit major life activities. In addition, each of the 50 states and U.S. territories has statutes that protect the rights of students in elementary and secondary schools.

The Individuals With Disabilities Education Act

In 1975 Congress passed, and President Gerald Ford signed, landmark legislation then known as the Education for All Handicapped Children Act (1975). That statute, which was renamed the IDEA in 1990 (and for the sake of clarity, this is the title that will be used in this book), mandates a free appropriate public education (FAPE) in the least restrictive environment (LRE) for all students with disabilities between the ages of 3 and 21, inclusive (20 U.S.C. § 1412(a)(1)(A)), unless this age-range provision is inconsistent with state law (20 U.S.C. § 1412(a)(1)(B)(i)). The IDEA further provides an exception to the obligation to provide services to youth between the ages of 18 through 21 who are incarcerated if they were not identified as having disabilities or did not have IEPs prior to their incarceration (20 U.S.C. § 1412(a)(1)(B)(ii)). A FAPE is defined as special education and related services that are provided at public expense, meet state educational standards, include an appropriate preschool, elementary, or secondary school education, and are provided in conformity with an IEP (20 U.S.C. § 1401(9)). The IDEA's LRE provision states that

> to the maximum extent appropriate, children with disabilities . . . are educated with children who are not disabled, and special classes, separate schooling, or other removal of children with disabilities from the regular educational environment occurs only when the nature or severity of the disability of a child is such that education in regular classes with the use of supplementary aids and services cannot be achieved satisfactorily. (20 U.S.C. § 1412(a)(5))

The term *children with disabilities,* as defined in the statute, includes those with mental retardation, hearing impairments, speech or language impairments, visual impairments, serious emotional disturbance, orthopedic impairments, autism, traumatic brain injury, other health impairments, or specific learning disabilities who need special education and related services (20 U.S.C. § 1401(3)).

The IDEA gives students with disabilities, and their parents, many due process rights that are unprecedented in the history of education law.

Students' rights under the IDEA include opportunities to have disputes over the provision of a FAPE brought to independent hearing officers and eventually to the courts (20 U.S.C. § 1415(f)-(i)). Further, the IDEA requires states, and by delegation school boards and local school officials, to develop IEPs for all students who need special education. The IDEA defines *special education* as specially designed instruction to meet students' unique needs that is provided at no cost to their parents (20 U.S.C. § 1401(29)).

According to the IDEA, school officials must develop IEPs in concert with the students' parents. At a minimum, IEPs must include statements of students' current levels of educational performance, measurable annual goals and short-term objectives, statements of the special education and related services or program modifications students are to receive, explanations of the extent to which students are to participate in regular classroom activities, statements concerning modifications required for statewide or districtwide assessments, the dates covered by the IEPs, and the criteria by which progress toward annual goals will be measured. When students turn 16, their IEPs must include transition plans to address what they will do when they complete their formal schooling (20 U.S.C. § 1414(d)).

Since 1975, the statute has been subject to significant amendments. One of the amendments, enacted in 1990, changed the name of the statute to its current title and updated much of its terminology. As initially enacted and amended, the statute did not specifically mention discipline. Yet, many of the IDEA's provisions were applied to the disciplinary process for students with disabilities. In view of the fact that serious disciplinary sanctions, such as expulsions, cause deprivations of educational opportunities, and consequently deprivations of rights granted in the IDEA, courts recognized that students with disabilities had additional due process rights when faced with such disciplinary actions.

In 1997, when Congress passed a comprehensive amendment to the IDEA, it specifically included provisions governing the disciplinary process for students with disabilities (20 U.S.C. § 1415(k); 34 C.F.R. §§ 300.530–537). Many of those provisions simply codified existing case law. However, other provisions helped to clarify gray areas that previously existed. The IDEA's disciplinary requirements were further refined in an amendment passed in 2004. These mandates are discussed at greater length later in this chapter. The disciplinary sections of the IDEA apply to summer school programs as well as to school year programs (*L. I. H. ex rel. L. H. v. New York City Board of Education*, 2000).

The IDEA's current disciplinary provisions have been reproduced in Resource A. The pertinent implementing regulations from the Code of Federal Regulations have been reproduced in Resource B.

Section 504 of the Rehabilitation Act

Section 504 was the first federal civil rights law protecting the rights of individuals with disabilities. Modeled after other civil rights laws, Section 504 simply states that "no otherwise qualified individual with a disability in the United States . . . shall, solely by reason of her or his disability, be excluded from the participation in, be denied the benefits of, or be subjected to discrimination under any program or activity receiving federal financial assistance. . . ." (29 U.S.C. § 794(a)). Section 504 defines an individual with a disability as one "who (i) has a physical or mental impairment which substantially limits one or more of such person's major life activities, (ii) has a record of such an impairment, or (iii) is regarded as having such an impairment" (29 U.S.C. § 706(7)(B)).

In addition to prohibiting discriminatory treatment, Section 504 requires school officials to make reasonable accommodations for students with disabilities. This means that educators must provide any aid, benefits, and/or services that are comparable to those available to students who do not have disabilities. As such, students with disabilities must receive comparable materials, teacher quality, length of school term, and daily hours of instruction. Reasonable accommodations may involve minor adjustments such as allowing physically challenged students additional time to change classes, permitting students to be accompanied by service dogs, or providing hearing interpreters for students. Academic modifications might include giving students longer periods of time to complete examinations or assignments, using peer tutors, distributing outlines in advance, employing specialized curricular materials, and/or permitting students to use laptop computers to record answers on examinations.

> In addition to prohibiting discriminatory treatment, Section 504 requires school officials to make reasonable accommodations for students with disabilities.

Like the IDEA, Section 504's regulations require school boards to provide students with disabilities with a FAPE (34 C.F.R. § 104.33(a)). An appropriate education under Section 504 may include regular or special education and related services (34 C.F.R. § 104.33(b)(1)). Although implementation of an IEP under the IDEA would satisfy this requirement (34 C.F.R. § 104.33(b)(2)), not all students with disabilities require special education. This is a major difference between the two statutes. The IDEA stipulates that students with disabilities must require special education to come within the act's provisions (20 U.S.C. § 1401(3)(A)(ii)). To this end, since some students with disabilities may not receive services under the IDEA and are not protected by its procedures, they may still be safeguarded by Section 504.

Section 504 dictates that programs for students with disabilities should not be separate from those available to students who do not have disabilities, unless such segregation is necessary for the program to be effective. While school officials are not prohibited from offering separate programs for students with disabilities, such students cannot be required to attend segregated classes unless they cannot be served adequately in the regular educational setting (34 C.F.R. § 104.4(b)(3)). When programs are offered separately, facilities must, of course, be comparable to those used by students who do not have disabilities (34 C.F.R. § 104.34(c)).

Unlike the IDEA's regulations, Section 504's regulations do not contain specific disciplinary requirements. However, in light of the history of case law that existed under the IDEA prior to the passage of the disciplinary amendments, it is reasonable to assume that similar procedures should be put in place for students who come within the ambit of Section 504 only. In fact, as is discussed in later chapters, the U.S. Department of Education and the courts have interpreted Section 504's regulations as requiring additional procedural protections.

The Americans With Disabilities Act

The ADA prohibits discrimination against individuals with disabilities in the private as well as the public sector. The purpose of the ADA is to provide a clear and comprehensive national mandate for the elimination of discrimination against individuals with disabilities (42 U.S.C. § 12101). One of the ADA's primary intents was to extend the protections afforded by Section 504 to programs and activities that are not covered by the latter statute because they do not receive federal funds. The ADA contains provisions similar to those of Section 504 regarding reasonable accommodations.

The ADA is aimed primarily at the private sector. Even so, public agencies are not immune from the ADA's provisions (Wenkart, 1993). In educational institutions, compliance with Section 504 generally translates to compliance with the ADA because of their similarities (Miles, Russo, & Gordon, 1991). In fact, the disposition of claims filed under both statutes is generally identical for each statute. However, this does

> The ADA is aimed primarily at the private sector. Even so, public agencies are not immune from the ADA's provisions.

not automatically mean that compliance with Section 504 is tantamount to compliance with the ADA, because the legislative history of the ADA indicates that it addresses what the judiciary perceived as shortcomings or loopholes in Section 504 (Osborne, 1995).

The ADA's impact on students is most noteworthy in the area of reasonable accommodations in academic programs. While schools are subject to many similar regulations under Section 504, conformity with the latter act in this regard should ensure compliance with the former. In other words, if schools have realistically implemented Section 504 and its regulations, they should not have compliance difficulties with the ADA. School personnel can avoid difficulties with the ADA by implementing proactive policies and procedures to provide reasonable accommodations when needed.

The ADA includes five major sections known as Titles, the first three of which have significant implications for public schools. As such, they receive the lion's share of this analysis.

Title I covers employment in the private sector and is directly applicable to private schools. Title I requires school personnel to make reasonable accommodations for otherwise qualified individuals once officials are aware of the individuals' impairments. This means that in order to be covered by the ADA, employees need to inform school authorities of their conditions along with specific suggestions on how their needs can be met.

In its first revision of the statute, Congress enacted the ADA Amendments Act of 2008 explicitly abrogating the Supreme Court's rulings in *Sutton v. United Air Lines* (*Sutton*, 1999) and *Toyota Motor Manufacturing, Kentucky v. Williams* (*Toyota*, 2002), cases that reduced the protections that Congress intended to provide for employees. More specifically, in *Sutton*, the Court maintained that since persons with mental or physical impairments that could be corrected through the use of medication or other steps did not have impairments that presently limited major life activities, they were not protected by the ADA. Further, in *Toyota*, the Court was of the opinion that the term "substantially limits" meant that in order to be covered by the ADA, impairments had to prevent or severely restrict individuals from taking part in activities of central importance to the daily lives of most people, highlighting the notion that the impact of impairments must be permanent or long term before persons are entitled to protection under the Act.

The revised ADA expands the definition of disability, making it easier for individuals to prove that they were subjected to workplace discrimination, especially if they suffered from epilepsy, diabetes, cancer, multiple sclerosis, or other ailments and were improperly denied protection insofar as their conditions could be controlled by medications or other measures.

At the same time, the amended act changes Section 504 so that the definitions of disability and major life activities in both laws will be the same.

Title II applies to the public services of state and local governments for both employers and providers, including transportation, and especially education, because part of this Title applies to public schools.

Title III is concerned with public accommodations. By covering both the private and public sectors, Title III expands the scope of Section 504. Title III includes private businesses and a wide array of community services, including buildings, transportation systems, parks, recreational facilities, hotels, and theaters. Title IV addresses telecommunications, specifically voice and nonvoice systems.

Title V contains the ADA's miscellaneous provisions. These parts of the law stipulate both that the ADA cannot be construed as applying a lesser standard than would be applied under Section 504 and its regulations, and that qualified individuals are not required to accept services that fall short of meeting their needs.

State Laws

Insofar as education is a function of the states, special education is governed by both state laws and the federal statutes discussed above. Each state's special education and antidiscrimination laws must be consistent with the federal statutes, but differences do exist. While most states have laws that are similar in scope, and even language, to the IDEA, several have provisions in their legislation that go beyond the IDEA's requirements, thereby providing additional rights and privileges to students with disabilities. Other states have stricter procedural requirements. Most have established procedures for program implementation that are either uncovered by federal law or have been left to the states to determine for themselves. If a conflict develops between provisions of the federal law and a state law, the federal law is supreme. Although a review of each state's special education and antidiscrimination laws is beyond the scope of this book, readers are advised to check their own state's provisions, as they may have an effect on the disciplinary process.

> While most states have laws that are similar in scope, and even language, to the IDEA, several have provisions in their legislation that go beyond the IDEA's requirements, thereby providing additional rights and privileges to students with disabilities.

EARLY CASE LAW

As indicated above, the IDEA initially did not contain any provisions that directly addressed disciplinary situations. Still, courts often were called on to settle disputes arising out of disciplinary actions. A large body of case law developed from these lawsuits. Even though much of this case law has been superseded by the 1997 and 2004 IDEA amendments, an analysis of the case law can be instructive, as many of the current provisions are little more than a codification of the case law.

The First Lower Court Decisions

Expulsion Is a Change in Placement

It should not be surprising that the first court case decided under the IDEA involved discipline. *Stuart v. Nappi* (*Stuart*, 1978) involved school officials' attempt to expel a student with disabilities who was involved in schoolwide disturbances. The student's attorney requested a due process hearing under the IDEA and obtained a temporary restraining order from the federal trial court in Connecticut that prevented the school board from conducting a hearing to expel the student. When it ruled on the merits, the court declared that an expulsion was a change in placement that was not consistent with the IDEA's procedures. Specifically, the court cited a section of the law that provides that written prior notice must be given to students' parents when school boards propose to change students' educational placements (20 U.S.C. § 1415(b)(3)).

> It should not be surprising that the first court case decided under the IDEA involved discipline.

In *Stuart*, the court noted that if parents object to changes and request due process hearings, the IDEA prohibits school boards from making those changes during the pendency of any proceedings under the so-called stay-put provision (20 U.S.C. § 1415(j)). Although the court found the attempted expulsion to be problematic under the IDEA, it did concede that school officials could temporarily suspend disruptive special education students or change their placements to more restrictive ones by following the act's procedures. Three years later, in an unpublished opinion, the same court handed down a similar decision in a case that was procedurally identical to *Stuart*. The court reiterated that officials could not circumvent the IDEA's procedures when taking disciplinary action (*Blue v. New Haven Board of Education*, 1981).

Short-Term Suspensions

Courts in other jurisdictions agreed that students with disabilities could be subjected to short-term suspensions. In *Board of Education of Peoria v. Illinois State Board of Education* (1982), a federal trial court upheld a school's five-day suspension of a special education student. The court ruled that a brief period of forced absence, such as a five-day suspension, could not reasonably be considered a change in placement. In reviewing a case from Arkansas, *Wise v. Pea Ridge School District* (1988), the Eighth Circuit affirmed that a three-day in-house suspension, even when the student was denied access to his special education teacher and resources, did not violate the student's substantive due process rights under the IDEA because he continued to receive educational services.

Manifestation of the Disability Doctrine

Shortly after *Stuart,* a federal trial court in Indiana determined that school officials could not expel students with disabilities whose disruptive conduct was caused by their disabilities (*Doe v. Koger,* 1979). This became known as the "manifestation of the disability" doctrine and was later incorporated into the IDEA. However, the court left open the option that students with disabilities could be expelled when there was no relationship between their misconduct and their disabilities. The court reiterated that special education students who are disruptive may be transferred to more restrictive placements as long as officials follow proper change in placement procedures. Even so, in *Victoria L. v. District School Board of Lee County* (1984), the Eleventh Circuit upheld a school board in Florida's transfer of a student, who brought a razor blade and martial arts weapons to school and threatened to injure or kill another student, to an alternative school over her mother's objection. The court agreed that the evidence failed to demonstrate in any way that the placement was inappropriate under the circumstances.

The Fifth Circuit extended the manifestation of the disability doctrine in *S-1 v. Turlington* (*Turlington,* 1981), another case from Florida. (Authors' note: At that time Florida was in the Fifth Circuit. The Fifth Circuit was split in October 1981, and Florida is now in the Eleventh Circuit). In *Turlington* students faced expulsion for a variety of acts of misconduct. One of the students requested a hearing to evaluate whether his misconduct was a manifestation of his disability. The superintendent of schools maintained that since the student was not classified as emotionally disturbed, his misconduct was not a manifestation of his disability. In overturning the expulsion, the Fifth Circuit ruled that a manifestation decision must be made by a specialized and knowledgeable group of persons. Even in situations where officials agree that there is no relationship between students' misconduct and their disabilities, and they are properly expelled consistent with the IDEA's procedures, the court concluded that there still could not be a complete cessation of services. A year later, in a case from Kentucky, the Sixth Circuit adopted the analysis from *Turlington* (*Kaelin v. Grubbs,* 1982).

A decision of the Fourth Circuit reveals that it was not always difficult to demonstrate that a relationship existed between students' disabilities and their misconduct. In *School Board of the County of Prince William v. Malone* (1985), a student from Virginia who was classified as learning disabled was involved in several drug transactions. A committee of special education professionals met and determined that since there was no causal relationship between the student's disabilities and his involvement in the drug transactions, he could be expelled. However, the court found that a relationship did, in fact, exist, because the student's learning disability gave him a poor self-image, which caused him to seek peer approval by becoming involved in the drug transactions. Moreover, the court thought that his learning disability prevented him from understanding the long-term consequences of his actions. The Fourth Circuit affirmed that insofar as the student's expulsion for a drug violation that was related to his disability was not clearly erroneous, there was no reason to disturb the trial court's order.

Exclusion of Dangerous Students

Even under early case law, school officials were allowed to exclude students who posed a danger to others, as long as the authorities followed proper procedures. For example, the Fifth Circuit upheld a Mississippi school board's exclusion of a student who was diagnosed as having a psychosexual disorder (*Jackson v. Franklin County School Board*, 1985). The student was committed to a state hospital for treatment by the youth court, but when he tried to return to school after being released from the hospital, educational personnel refused to admit him. Instead, educators recommended that the student be placed in a private facility. The court supported the right of school officials to exclude a student they considered to be dangerous.

U.S. Supreme Court Decision

In 1988 the U.S. Supreme Court affirmed that students with disabilities could not be expelled for misconduct that was a manifestation of their disabilities. *Honig v. Doe* (*Honig*, 1988) involved two special education students identified in court documents as John Doe and Jack Smith. Doe, an emotionally disturbed student who had aggressive tendencies, attended a developmental center for students with disabilities. Shortly after he was placed at the school, Doe assaulted another student and broke a school window. Doe was suspended for five days and then placed on an indefinite suspension pending an expulsion hearing. Doe's attorney requested that the expulsion hearing be

> In 1988 the U.S. Supreme Court affirmed that students with disabilities could not be expelled for misconduct that was a manifestation of their disabilities.

canceled and that the IEP team be convened. Court action was initiated when school officials ignored that request. Eventually, the board cancelled the expulsion hearing and the trial court issued a temporary restraining order to readmit Doe to school. The court later issued a preliminary injunction to prevent school authorities from excluding Doe while they searched for an alternative placement.

Smith, who was also emotionally disturbed with aggressive tendencies, was placed in a special education setting in a regular school on a trial basis. Yet, school personnel reduced Smith's program to a half-day schedule after he was involved in a number of incidents of misconduct. Although Smith's grandparents, who served as his guardians, agreed to this change, they were not advised of their rights or options regarding his IEP. Smith was later given a five-day suspension, and school officials recommended his expulsion after he made sexual comments to female students. Officials continued Smith's suspension pending resolution of his expulsion proceedings. Smith's attorney objected to the expulsion hearing. Consequently, school officials canceled the proceedings and offered either to restore the half-day program or provide home tutoring. Smith's grandparents chose the home tutoring option. A federal trial court in California later held that a reduction in schedule without first convening the IEP team violated the IDEA (*Doe v. Maher*, 1984).

The trial court and the Ninth Circuit both ruled that students with disabilities could not be expelled for behavior that was related to their disabilities (*Doe v. Maher*, 1984, 1986). The Supreme Court affirmed, with Justice Brennan emphatically stating that Congress intended to limit school officials' power to exclude students with disabilities, even for disciplinary purposes:

> We think it clear, however, that Congress very much meant to strip schools of the *unilateral* authority they had traditionally employed to exclude disabled students, particularly emotionally disturbed students, from school. In so doing, Congress did not leave school administrators powerless to deal with dangerous students; it did, however, deny school officials their former right to "self help," and directed that in the future the removal of disabled students could be accomplished only with the permission of the parents or, as a last resort, the courts. (pp. 323–324)

Honig did not leave school officials without recourse. In its majority opinion the Court pointed out that school officials could temporarily suspend students with disabilities for up to 10 school days if the students posed an immediate threat to the safety of others. During the 10-day "cooling off" period, the Court indicated that school officials should try to reach agreement with students' parents for alternate placements. However, in situations where the parents adamantly refuse to consent to a change in placement, the Court maintained that school officials could request the aid of the courts. In such circumstances, the Court reasoned that school officials would not be required to exhaust administrative remedies prior to filing judicial action if they could show that administrative review was futile or inadequate. Under the IDEA's elaborate due process scheme, parties to a special education dispute normally must exhaust all administrative remedies prior to filing a lawsuit in the courts (20 U.S.C § 1415(i)).

In its analysis in *Honig*, the high Court added that in appropriate cases, the lower courts could temporarily enjoin dangerous students from attending school. On the other hand, the Court remarked that the IDEA created a presumption in favor of students' current educational placements and that educational officials could overcome this presumption only by showing that preserving the status quo was substantially likely to result in injury to that child or other students. Thus, according to the Court, the burden was on school officials to demonstrate that students were dangerous and that no alternatives remained other than exclusion from students' former placements in order to mitigate the danger that they presented. An edited version of the Supreme Court's *Honig* opinion is reproduced in Resource C for readers who would like to read the original order in the Court's own words.

> The court remarked that the IDEA created a presumption in favor of students' current educational placements and that educational officials could overcome this presumption only by showing that preserving the status quo was substantially likely to result in injury to that child or other students.

Post-*Honig* Decisions

Honig clarified many issues regarding the discipline of special education students. Even so, litigation continued. *Honig* made it clear that students with disabilities could not be expelled for behavior that was related to their disabilities. However, the Court was of the view that school officials could employ other normal disciplinary sanctions that did not result in changes in placements, such as short-term suspensions of less than 10 days.

Time-Outs and Detentions

About a year after *Honig* was resolved, the Tenth Circuit, in reversing a judgment of the federal trial court in Kansas, acknowledged that short-term disciplinary measures do not constitute a change in placement under the IDEA (*Hayes v. Unified School District No. 377*, 1989). The parents of two students with histories of academic and behavior problems contested the use of in-school suspensions and time-outs. Time-out is a common tool used in many special education classrooms whereby students are placed in isolated areas (generally within their classrooms) until they can return to the larger groups without disruption. Although the court held that such short-term measures did not amount to changes in placement, it did observe that they were a matter relating to the education of the students and thus were subject to the IDEA's administrative due process procedures. Similarly, a trial court in North Carolina, citing *Honig*, ruled that a 10-day suspension did not violate the IDEA's stay-put provision (*Glen III v. Charlotte-Mecklenburg School Board of Education*, 1995).

Injunctions

In *Honig*, the Supreme Court envisioned that the cooling off period provided via short-term suspensions would allow school officials and parents to work together to devise other placements for students when they were needed. Unfortunately, though, school officials and parents do not always agree, and other options cannot always be developed during that 10-day period. Normally, when parents and school officials are unable to reach agreement, their disputes are subject to the often-lengthy administrative and judicial process. Still, *Honig* granted school officials the ability to seek injunctions to remove students with disabilities who were either dangerous or created serious disruptions to the educational process while administrative and judicial proceedings were pending. When such actions occur, *Honig* placed the burden on school officials to show that the students were truly dangerous and that removal from their then-current educational placement was the only feasible option.

> *Honig* granted school officials the ability to seek injunctions to remove students with disabilities who were either dangerous or created serious disruptions to the educational process while administrative and judicial proceedings were pending.

Early courts settled numerous suits involving requests for *Honig* injunctions. These judicial opinions offer a better understanding of the situations in which injunctions may be granted. In one case, a state court in Virginia granted an injunction to exclude a 12-year-old student who was involved in fights, struck and yelled obscenities at school officials, and often had to be restrained by the police (*School Board of the County of Prince William v. Wills*, 1989). A year later, another state court in Virginia issued an injunction against a student who set a fire in a school locker, among other infractions (*School Board of the County of Stafford v. Farley*, 1990). In yet another situation, a federal trial court in Illinois issued an injunction barring a student who violently struck peers while also threatening to kill other students and staff

(*Board of Education of Township High School District v. Kurtz-Imig*, 1989). In New York, a state court concluded that school officials met their burden of showing that a student, who ran out of the school waving an iron bar while threatening to kill someone, was likely to endanger other students if he returned to school (*East Islip Union Free School District v. Andersen*, 1994).

Other cases showed that a history of serious misbehavior alone was not always sufficient to obtain *Honig* injunctions. For example, a trial court in Missouri refused to issue an injunction to exclude a student who made repeated threats to classmates and school officials, repeatedly exploded in anger, and threw furniture (*Clinton County R-III School District v. C. J. K.*, 1995). Even though another child was injured during one of these incidents, and teachers testified that they were afraid of him, the court decided that this was insufficient to establish that serious personal injury was likely to occur if the student remained in his then-current placement. Similarly, a federal trial court in Pennsylvania refused to issue an injunction when school officials were unable to demonstrate that they had taken every reasonable measure to mitigate the danger posed by a student who cut the hand of another student with a razor (*School District of Philadelphia v. Stephan M. and Theresa M.*, 1997). The student in this case alleged that she acted as she did because the victim exposed himself to her and tried to fondle her.

Alternative Placements

In other cases, courts not only issued injunctions to bar students from attending school in their former placements but also ordered alternative placements. A federal trial court in Texas issued an injunction prohibiting a student, who had assaulted peers and teachers, destroyed school property, used profanity, and threatened to kill himself and others, from attending general education classes (*Texas City Independent School District v. Jorstad*, 1990). The student's parents rejected school officials' recommendation that their son be placed in a special education behavior management class. The court issued an order directing that the student could either attend the behavior management class or receive home tutoring pending completion of the administrative review process. Likewise, a federal trial court in New York issued an injunction that placed a student in a special education class pending completion of a due process hearing (*Binghamton City School District v. Borgna*, 1991). The student had exhibited aggressive behavior such as punching peers, sticking a pencil in another child's ear, throwing his shoes at staff, hitting faculty, tipping over desks, and throwing chairs. In still another case, a federal trial court in Florida granted an injunction allowing school personnel to transfer a student to a special education center after he was involved in 43 instances of aggressive behavior (*School Board of Pinellas County v. J. M. by L. M.*, 1997).

The Eighth Circuit provided excellent guidance concerning when students with disabilities can be removed from their current educational settings. In *Light v. Parkway C-2 School District* (1994), a case from Missouri, the court allowed school officials to remove a student with mental disabilities, who exhibited a steady stream of aggressive and disruptive behaviors, from her special education placement. The court explained that even a child whose behaviors flow directly from her disabilities is subject to removal if she poses a substantial risk of injury to herself or others. At the same time, the court commented that in addition to showing that the student presented such a danger, school personnel must also demonstrate that they made a reasonable effort to accommodate her disabilities and minimize the likelihood that she would injure herself or others. The court emphasized that only a showing of the likelihood of injury was required: A child need not inflict serious harm on herself or others before being deemed likely to cause injury. Further, the court decreed that injury is not defined solely as an infliction that draws blood or sends the victim to an emergency room but includes bruises, bites, and poked eyes.

Students Not Yet Identified as Having Disabilities

Another issue that developed in the post-*Honig* era was whether students who had not yet been identified as having disabilities were entitled to the protections of the IDEA if they claimed to have unidentified disabilities at the time they committed their acts of misconduct. In reviewing a case from California, the Ninth Circuit expressed the view that *Honig* indicated that all students with disabilities, regardless of whether they had previously been identified as disabled, were entitled to the procedural protections of the IDEA (*Hacienda La Puente Unified School District of Los Angeles v. Honig*, 1992). Similarly, a federal trial court in California found that the IDEA's procedural safeguards must be applied regardless of whether students were previously diagnosed as having disabilities (*M. P. by D. P. v. Governing Board of the Grossmont Union High School District*, 1994). The court recognized that a student who did not have disabilities could attempt to be labeled as disabled solely to gain the benefits of the IDEA, but it stated that the statute (at that time) did not address this possibility.

On the other hand, a federal trial court in Virginia pointed out that a student who was suspended for handling a loaded handgun on school property was not entitled to the protections of the IDEA because she failed to raise the question of her disability until well after the incident that led to her suspension occurred (*Doe v. Manning*, 1994). In a situation involving a student from Ohio who faced expulsion after he had been referred for a special education evaluation but before the evaluation was completed, the

Sixth Circuit stated that to allow the student to utilize IDEA safeguards and benefits before an actual diagnosis of disability would be premature and would take resources away from students who had been diagnosed as disabled (*Doe v. Board of Education of the Elyria City Schools*, 1998). The court noted, however, that in this case, once the student had been diagnosed, his expulsion was revoked.

One factor in determining disability relatedness, which was later incorporated into the IDEA, was whether school authorities knew, or had reason to know, that the students did, in fact, have disabilities. For example, the federal trial court in Minnesota was of the opinion that a student who had not been assessed as being disabled could assert the procedural protections of the IDEA because evidence revealed that school officials were aware that he might have a disability (*J. B. v. Independent School District No. 191, Burnsville*, 1995). Part of that persuasive evidence, in the court's view, was the fact that the student was failing all of his courses. In another case, the same court concluded that a student who was diagnosed as having significant language delays by a private facility, but not by the school board's assessment team, was entitled to the IDEA's protections, because educational personnel had a copy of the evaluation report, and thus had reason to know that he required special education (*Davis v. Independent School District No. 196, Rosemount–Apple Valley–Eagan Schools*, 1996).

Students No Longer Receiving Special Education

A related issue is whether former special education students, who were not receiving special education and related services at the time of the disciplinary infractions, were entitled to the protections of the IDEA. A decision by a federal trial court in Wisconsin indicates that the answer is "yes," especially, as in this situation, if the students were removed from special education at the request of their parents but school officials had not determined that they no longer required special education services (*Steldt v. School Board of the Riverdale School District*, 1995). In this case, the student was removed from a special education class for emotionally disturbed students at his mother's request but against the recommendation of his teacher. The student was later expelled for a series of acts that included assaults on fellow students, a teacher, and the principal. In acknowledging that the student was entitled to the protections of the IDEA, the court emphasized that his mother's request to remove her son from a special education placement did not change his status as a student in need of special education. Thus, the court was convinced that the student was still a student with disabilities entitled to the protections of the IDEA.

Students Determined to Not Have Disabilities

Another issue along the same line is how to treat students who were evaluated but found ineligible for IDEA services. As with many issues, the answer may well be resolved by the unique facts of a case. In one instance, where school personnel in Illinois thought that a student did not require special education, his mother contested their judgment (*Rodiriecus L. v. Waukegan School District No. 60,* 1996). The Seventh Circuit decreed that the student was not entitled to an injunction barring his expulsion while administrative proceedings were pending. The court indicated that under these circumstances, a flexible approach to applying the IDEA's stay-put provision was needed, and it should not automatically have been applied to every student who filed an application for special education.

Consecutive or Cumulative Suspension Days

According to *Honig,* special education students may be suspended for up to 10 days. However, the Supreme Court failed to address whether that 10-day limit was consecutive or cumulative. In other words, it was unclear whether students who received 10-day suspensions could be suspended again later that same school year. The Ninth Circuit was convinced that the high Court's opinion did not support the argument that the 10-day limit referred to 10 total days (*Parents of Student W. v. Puyallup School District,* 1994). The court ascertained that the suspension guidelines of a school board in Washington, which dictated that each suspension trigger an evaluation to determine whether the student was receiving an appropriate education, were lawful. Conversely, the federal trial court in New Hampshire decided that cumulative suspensions that totaled more than 10 days constituted a pattern of exclusion that resulted in a change of placement (*Manchester School District v. Charles M. F.,* 1994).

Services During Expulsions

In its 1981 judgment in *S-1 v. Turlington,* discussed earlier, the Fifth Circuit ruled that even when special education students are properly expelled by following all of the IDEA's due process procedures, the act did not authorize a complete cessation of services. Pursuant to *Turlington,* school boards still needed to provide special education and related services to students with disabilities who were expelled for misbehavior. Sixteen years later, the federal trial court in Arizona agreed (*Magyar v. Tucson Unified School District,* 1997). In granting a student's motion for summary judgment after he was expelled for a weapon violation, the court noted that the IDEA requires school boards to provide an appropriate education for all students with disabilities. The court believed that since the use of the word *all* in the IDEA was clear and unequivocal, it did not include an exception for misbehaving students.

Not all early courts agreed. In 1992, when commonwealth officials in Virginia submitted their three-year plan for special education to the U.S. Department of Education, it included a regulation stating that students with disabilities could be disciplined in the same manner as peers who are not disabled if there was no causal relationship between their misconduct and their disabilities. The U.S. Department of Education responded by notifying Virginia that it could not discontinue educational services to expelled special education students even when the discipline resulted from behavior unrelated to the students' disabilities. Virginia failed to change the regulation and the dispute eventually ended up in the courts.

After much litigation, the Fourth Circuit, sitting *en banc,* meaning that all of the appeals court judges in the circuit had the opportunity to participate in the decision, in *Commonwealth of Virginia Department of Education v. Riley* (1997), decided that the IDEA did not require local school boards to discipline students with disabilities, whose misconduct was unrelated to their impairments, differently from students who did not have disabilities. The court found that the IDEA only requires jurisdictions to provide students with disabilities with access to a FAPE, and, as with any right, that right of access could be forfeited by conduct antithetical to the right itself. The court thus ruled that school boards were not required to provide educational services to students with disabilities who forfeited the right to a FAPE by willfully engaging in conduct so serious as to warrant the ultimate discipline of expulsion.

Several months later, the Seventh Circuit reached a similar outcome in a case from Illinois involving a student who was expelled for possession of a pipe and a small amount of marijuana (*Doe v. Board of Education of Oak Park & River Forest High School District 200,* 1997). The trial court held that the school board was not required to provide alternative educational services during the expulsion period. The appellate court affirmed, explaining that the IDEA was not intended to shield special education students from the usual consequences of misconduct when that misconduct was not related to their disabilities. These cases stood in direct contrast to opinion letters issued by the U.S. Department of Education (*Boggus Letter,* 1993; *Davis Letter,* 1989; *Hartman Letter,* 1995; *New Letter,* 1989; *Price Letter,* 1993; *Smith Letter,* 1992; *Symkowick Letter,* 1991; *Taylor Letter,* 1993; *Uhler Letter,* 1992). Again, this is an issue that was settled by the passage of the 1997 IDEA amendments.

AMENDMENTS TO THE IDEA

As indicated above, prior to 1997 the IDEA did not contain language specifically outlining the circumstances under which students with disabilities could be disciplined; neither did the act address what kinds of sanctions school officials could apply. Following a great deal of controversy, Congress added specific disciplinary provisions to the IDEA in 1997. These provisions were refined when Congress again amended the statute in 2004.

IDEA Amendments of 1997

Against the backdrop of an extensive body of case law, in the IDEA amendments of 1997, Congress implemented the most far-reaching changes to the federal special education law since it was originally enacted in 1975. For the first time in the IDEA's history, Congress included specific mandates for disciplining students with disabilities. As indicated above, while some of these provisions simply codified existing case law, many sections clarified some of the ambiguous areas that existed, and some even settled disagreements that had existed among the jurisdictions.

> For the first time in the IDEA's history, Congress included specific mandates for disciplining students with disabilities.

Among the major mandates in the IDEA's 1997 amendments was the incorporation of the judicial requirement that educators had to make manifestation determinations when disciplining students with disabilities. Yet, the amendment went further than the case law in spelling out the procedures that educators had to follow in making manifestation determinations (20 U.S.C. § 1415(k)(1)(E); 34 C.F.R. § 300.530(e)). The amendments also included a stipulation giving parents the right to expedited hearings to contest manifestation determinations (20 U.S.C. § 1415(k)(3); 34 C.F.R. § 300.532(c)). Although these provisions were modified with the enactment of the 2004 IDEA amendments, it is important to note that the statute currently prescribes the procedures that should be followed in making the manifestation determination.

As was shown above, it was well settled under case law that school officials could suspend students with disabilities for up to 10 school days. The 1997 amendments incorporated this aspect of the case law (20 U.S.C. § 1415(k)(1)(B); 34 C.F.R. § 530(b)) but added that when students with disabilities are suspended beyond the 10-day limit, educators must conduct functional behavioral assessments (FBAs) and must take steps to address the students' misconduct (20 U.S.C. § 1415(k)(1)(D); 34 C.F.R. § 300.530(d)).

Honig granted school officials the option of seeking injunctions to bar students with disabilities from school if they deemed the students to be dangerous. Under the 1997 amendments, Congress granted school personnel the additional option of seeking orders from hearing officers to place students in alternative settings for periods of up to 45 school days (20 U.S.C. § 1415(k)(3)(B); 34 C.F.R. § 300.530(g)). Although the statute fails to specify the criteria for obtaining orders from hearing officers, the case law regarding court injunctions to remove dangerous students provides some guidelines. In such circumstances, the burden is likely to be on school officials to show that students are dangerous and that changes in placements are necessary.

The 1997 amendments ended the controversy that existed regarding whether school boards were required to provide educational services to students with disabilities who have been expelled. The amended IDEA made it clear that special education services must continue during expulsion periods (20 U.S.C. § 1412(a)(1)(A)). In addition, the amendments settled the controversy that existed over how students who have yet to be identified as disabled are to be treated. Under the current version of the IDEA, the statute's protections must be extended to any students if school officials knew, or should have known, that they had disabilities when they misbehaved (20 U.S.C. § 1415(k)(5)(A); 34 C.F.R. § 300.534). Under the IDEA, school personnel are considered to have known that students may have disabilities if their parents or teachers expressed concerns about them or if their parents requested that they undergo evaluations (20 U.S.C. § 1415(k)(5)(B); 34 C.F.R. § 300.534(b)).

IDEA Amendments of 2004

Congress again amended the IDEA in 2004 and in doing so refined the disciplinary provisions that it enacted in 1997. These changes gave school officials greater freedom to remove disruptive students with disabilities from classes when their behavior was unrelated to their disabilities (20 U.S.C. § 1415(k)(1); 34 C.F.R. § 300.530(a), (b)). Although the law still requires IEP teams to conduct manifestation determinations, the process requires that misconduct be directly related to students' disabilities before relationships can be found (20 U.S.C. § 1415(k)(1)(F); 34 C.F.R. § 300.530(e)(1)).

> These changes gave school officials greater freedom to remove disruptive students with disabilities from classes when their behavior was unrelated to their disabilities.

Further, when due process hearings are requested to challenge manifestation determinations, students must remain in their disciplinary placements until the hearing officers resolve the complaints (20 U.S.C. § 1415(k)(4); 34 C.F.R. § 300.533). Even so, special education students who are removed from general educational environments are still entitled to educational and related services in alternative settings (20 U.S.C. § 1415(k)(1)(D); 34 C.F.R. § 300.530(d)(1)(i)).

These amendments further expand the conditions under which students may be placed in alternative educational settings. Currently students who carry or possess weapons to or at schools, on school premises, or to or at school functions, or who knowingly possess or use illegal drugs or sell or solicit the sale of controlled substances while at school, on school premises, or at school functions, or who have inflicted serious bodily injury on other persons while at school, on school premises, or at school functions may be placed in such settings (20 U.S.C. § 1415(k)(1)(G); 34 C.F.R. § 300.530(g)).

Some frequently asked questions about the disciplinary provisions of the IDEA, Section 504, and the ADA are summarized in Figure 3.1.

Figure 3.1   Frequently Asked Questions

Q. Why was it necessary to include disciplinary provisions in the IDEA?

A. Prior to passing the original version of the IDEA in 1975, Congress found that far too many students with disabilities were not being given an adequate education. Many students with disabilities were totally excluded from the public schools. A majority of these students were considered to be difficult to maintain in educational settings, because their disabilities caused them to exhibit behavior problems. Even after the passage of the IDEA, case law indicated that some school boards tried to exclude students with disabilities who had behavior problems rather than provide them with the free appropriate public education to which they were entitled.

Q. Do the IDEA's disciplinary procedures provide a dual system of discipline—one for students with disabilities and one for those who do not have disabilities?

A. No. Students with disabilities are not immune from the disciplinary process, and the IDEA's procedures do not prevent students with disabilities from being properly disciplined. The IDEA's procedures create additional safeguards to make sure that students with disabilities are not denied the free appropriate public education to which they are entitled, particularly when their misconduct arises from their disabilities. Although almost all school administrators and school boards make concerted efforts to meet the educational needs of students with disabilities, unfortunately, due to the long history of exclusion, it is necessary for these additional protections to be in place.

Q. Section 504 and the ADA do not contain specific disciplinary provisions like those in the IDEA. Why is it necessary for school officials to consider these laws when disciplining students with disabilities?

A. Section 504 and the ADA are designed to prevent discrimination against individuals with disabilities. The regulations implementing these statutes also require school boards to provide students with disabilities with a FAPE. Although most students with disabilities come under the auspices of the IDEA, not all are covered by it. Nevertheless, these students are still covered by Section 504 and the ADA. In these cases, while the IDEA's procedures are not strictly applicable, school officials would be wise to provide students with additional procedural safeguards similar to those called for in the IDEA in order to avoid discrimination charges.

> **Q. Why are the disciplinary provisions of the 1997 and 2004 IDEA amendments significant?**
>
> **A.** Although much of what is contained in the current disciplinary sections of the IDEA and its regulations represents a codification of prior case law, these amendments are important for several reasons. First, the amendments made Congress's intent clear that students with disabilities were to be given additional protections as part of the disciplinary process. Additionally, insofar as courts in different jurisdictions issued some seemingly conflicting opinions, the amendments made the disciplinary procedures uniform across all jurisdictions. Finally, insofar as case law failed to address all possible situations, the amendments filled in the gaps by providing guidance on issues that had yet to be litigated.

SUMMARY

In 1975 Congress passed the original version of the IDEA to give states a federal mandate to provide students with disabilities with a free appropriate public education in the least restrictive environment. Although this law was passed, in part, to end the practice of excluding students who had behavior problems from the educational system, ironically it did not address the issue of disciplining students with disabilities. A large body of case law developed over disciplinary sanctions as applied to students with disabilities almost immediately following the statute's implementation.

Even though educators wisely rely largely on their attorneys when dealing with legal aspects of disciplining all students, particularly those in special education settings, they should acquaint themselves with both the federal and state legal systems. By familiarizing themselves with the legal systems of their home states, educators can greatly assist their attorneys and school boards, because such a working knowledge can help to cut right to the heart of issues and help to avoid unnecessary delays.

RECOMMENDATIONS FOR PRACTITIONERS

- Schedule regular professional development sessions for all professional staff and board members to help them to have a better understanding of how their legal systems operate and, more specifically, to recognize the significant differences and interplay between and among Section 504, the ADA, the IDEA, and other federal and state disability-related laws. Because the rules are fairly complicated (as demonstrated throughout this book), this will better serve the needs of children with disabilities and their parents, especially when these students are subjected to discipline.

- Provide similar informational sessions for parents and qualified students to help ensure that they are aware of their rights.
- Develop appropriate handout materials explaining in writing how various federal and state disability laws operate when it comes to disciplining students with disabilities.
- Make sure that all board policies and procedures relating to special education, particularly as matters relate to discipline, are up to date.
- Prepare checklists to help ensure that staff members are responding to parental requests in a timely and appropriate manner when questions of discipline arise.
- Consider the disciplinary rights of students who do not qualify for services under the IDEA but are covered by Section 504 and/or the ADA.
- Take steps to ensure that students with disabilities are not subjected to differential disciplinary treatment because of their disabilities.
- Ensure that compliance officers regularly monitor or audit educational programming to make sure that disciplinary, and all other, provisions comply with the dictates of Section 504, the IDEA, and other applicable federal and state laws.
- Recognize that in light of the complexity of disability law, it is important to rely on the advice of attorneys who specialize in education law. If school officials are unable to find such attorneys on their own, they should contact their state school board associations, bar associations, or professional groups such as the Education Law Association or National School Boards Association.

WHAT'S NEXT

Congress has added disciplinary provisions to the IDEA. These provisions codified much of the case law but also addressed other issues that had not been subject to litigation. Consequently, school officials now have a clear mandate on how to discipline students with disabilities. The next chapters analyze the IDEA's specific provisions and provide guidelines for its implementation.

REFERENCES

Americans with Disabilities Act (ADA), 42 U.S.C. §§ 12101–12213 (2006).
Americans with Disabilities Amendments Act of 2008, PL 110–325, 122 Stat. 3553 (2008).
Binghamton City School District v. Borgna, 17 EHLR 677 (N.D. N.Y. 1991).

Blue v. New Haven Board of Education, 3 EHLR 552:401 (D. Conn. 1981).

Board of Education of Peoria v. Illinois State Board of Education, 531 F. Supp. 148 (C.D. Ill. 1982).

Board of Education of Township High School District v. Kurtz-Imig, 16 EHLR 17 (N.D. Ill. 1989).

Boggus Letter, 20 IDELR 625 (OSEP 1993).

Clinton County R-III School District v. C. J. K., 896 F. Supp. 948 (W.D. Mo. 1995).

Code of Federal Regulations (C.F.R.), as cited.

Commonwealth of Virginia Department of Education v. Riley, 106 F.3d 559 (4th Cir. 1997).

Davis Letter, 16 EHLR 734 (OSERS 1989).

Davis v. Independent School District No. 196, Rosemount-Apple Valley-Eagan Schools, 23 IDELR 644 (D. Minn. 1996).

*Doe v. Board of Education of Oak Park & River Forest High School District 200,*115 F.3d 1273, (7th Cir. 1997).

Doe v. Board of Education of the Elyria City Schools, 1998 WL 344061 (6th Cir. 1998).

Doe v. Koger, 480 F. Supp. 225 (N.D. Ind. 1979).

Doe v. Maher, unpublished opinion (N.D. Cal. 1984), *affirmed in part, reversed in part, modified in part,* 793 F.2d 1470 (9th Cir. 1986), *affirmed sub nom. Honig v. Doe,* 484 U.S. 305 (1988).

Doe v. Manning, 1994 WL 99052 (W.D. Va. 1994).

East Islip Union Free School District v. Andersen, 615 N.Y.S.2d 852 (N.Y. Sup. Ct. 1994).

Education for All Handicapped Children Act, 20 U.S.C. § 1400 *et seq.* (1975).

Glen III v. Charlotte-Mecklenburg School Board of Education, 903 F. Supp. 918 (W.D. N.C. 1995).

Hacienda La Puente Unified School District of Los Angeles v. Honig, 976 F.2d 48 (9th Cir. 1992).

Hartman Letter, 23 IDELR 894 (OSEP 1995).

Hayes v. Unified School District No. 377, 877 F.2d 809 (10th Cir. 1989).

Honig v. Doe, 484 U.S. 305 (1988).

Individuals With Disabilities Education Act (IDEA), 20 U.S.C. §§ 1400–1482 (2006).

J. B. v. Independent School District No. 191, Burnsville, 21 IDELR 1157 (D. Minn. 1995).

Jackson v. Franklin County School Board, 765 F.2d 535 (5th Cir. 1985).

Kaelin v. Grubbs, 682 F.2d 595 (6th Cir. 1982).

L. I. H. ex rel. L. H. v. New York City Board of Education, 103 F. Supp.2d 658 (E.D. N.Y. 2000).

Light v. Parkway C-2 School District, 41 F.3d 1223 (8th Cir. 1994).

M. P. by D. P. v. Governing Board of the Grossmont Union High School District, 858 F. Supp. 1044 (S.D. Cal. 1994).

Magyar v. Tucson Unified School District, 958 F. Supp. 1423 (D. Ariz. 1997).

Manchester School District v. Charles M. F., 1994 WL 485754 (D. N.H. 1994).

Miles, A. S., Russo, C. J., & Gordon, W. M. (1991). The reasonable accommodations provisions of the Americans with Disabilities Act. *Education Law Reporter, 69,* 1–8.

New Letter, EHLR 213:258 (OSERS 1989).

Osborne, A. G. (1995). Court interpretations of the Americans with Disabilities Act and their effect on school districts. *Education Law Reporter, 95,* 489–498.

Parents of Student W. v. Puyallup School District, 31 F.3d 1489 (9th Cir. 1994).

Price Letter, 20 IDELR 1256 (OSERS 1993).

Rehabilitation Act, Section 504, 29 U.S.C. § 794 (2006).

Rodiriecus L. v. Waukegan School District No. 60, 90 F.3d 249 (7th Cir. 1996).

Russo, C. J., & Osborne, A. G. (2009). *Section 504 and the ADA*. Thousand Oaks, CA: Corwin.

S-1 v. Turlington, 635 F.2d 342 (5th Cir. 1981).

School Board of the County of Prince William v. Malone, 762 F.2d 1210 (4th Cir. 1985).

School Board of the County of Prince William v. Wills, 16 EHLR 1109 (Va. Cir. Ct. 1989).

School Board of the County of Stafford v. Farley, 16 EHLR 1119 (Va. Cir. Ct. 1990).

School Board of Pinellas County v. J. M. by L. M., 957 F. Supp. 1252 (M.D. Fla. 1997).

School District of Philadelphia v. Stephan M. and Theresa M., 1997 WL 89113 (E.D. Pa. 1997).

Smith Letter, 18 IDELR 685 (OSERS 1992).

Steldt v. School Board of the Riverdale School District, 885 F. Supp. 1192 (W.D. Wis. 1995).

Stuart v. Nappi, 443 F. Supp. 1235 (D. Conn. 1978).

Sutton v. United Air Lines, 527 U.S. 471 (1999).

Symkowick Letter, 17 EHLR 469 (OSERS 1991).

Taylor Letter, 20 IDELR 542 (OSERS 1993).

Texas City Independent School District v. Jorstad, 752 F. Supp. 231 (S.D. Tex. 1990).

Toyota Motor Manufacturing, Kentucky v. Williams, 534 U.S. 184 (2002).

Uhler Letter, 18 IDELR 1238 (OSEP 1992).

United States Code (U.S.C.), as cited.

Victoria L. v. District School Board of Lee County, 741 F.2d 369 (11th Cir. 1984).

Wenkart, R. D. (1993). The Americans with Disabilities Act and its impact on public education. *Education Law Reporter, 82*, 291–302.

Wise v. Pea Ridge School District, 855 F.2d 560 (8th Cir. 1988).

4 Removal of Students From General Educational Settings

INTRODUCTION

School administrators sometimes use suspensions and expulsions as disciplinary tools when students commit serious violations of school codes of conduct. Suspensions are generally defined as short-term removals from schools, while expulsions are usually long-term removals. In practice, suspensions generally are for 10 days or less. Expulsions may be for the remainder of the school term or longer, even permanent, depending on state law. As was shown in Chapter 2, any suspension of more than 10 days' duration procedurally should be treated in the same way as an expulsion.

Early case law and the current language of the Individuals with Disabilities Education Act (IDEA, 2006) indicate that students with disabilities may be suspended in the same manner as other students. Yet, students with disabilities may be expelled only after school officials provide them with additional due process safeguards. More specifically, one of the tasks school personnel must undertake prior to expelling students with disabilities is to evaluate whether their misbehaviors were caused by their disabilities. Even when students with disabilities are properly expelled under the IDEA, school officials must make provisions allowing them to continue to receive educational services.

This chapter presents information regarding the authority of school officials to discipline students with disabilities. The procedures that school personnel must follow in order to suspend or expel students with disabilities who have committed egregious acts of misconduct in accordance with the IDEA's dictates are discussed. The chapter includes an outline of the steps that individualized education program (IEP) teams must follow in considering whether student misbehaviors were caused by, or were manifestations of, their disabilities.

AUTHORITY OF SCHOOL PERSONNEL

In 2004 Congress inserted new language into the IDEA that affords school officials greater authority to consider unique circumstances on a case-by-case basis when contemplating changes in placement for students with disabilities who violate school rules (20 U.S.C. § 1415(k)(1)(A); 34 C.F.R. § 300.530(a)). In other words, the IDEA grants officials the authority to suspend students with disabilities or to remove them from their current educational settings to appropriate alternative settings for 10 days or less to the same extent that these sanctions would be applied to their peers who do not have disabilities (20 U.S.C. § 1415(k)(1)(B); 34 C.F.R. § 300.530(b)). School personnel also have the option of making placement changes in excess of 10 days when the misconduct that precipitates disciplinary action is determined not to be caused by students' disabilities (20 U.S.C. § 1415(k)(1)(C); 34 C.F.R. § 300.530(c)). Again, such actions must be taken in the same manner that they would be for students who do not have disabilities.

> School personnel also have the option of making placement changes in excess of 10 days when the misconduct that precipitates disciplinary action is determined not to be caused by students' disabilities.

FUNCTIONAL BEHAVIORAL ASSESSMENTS AND BEHAVIOR INTERVENTION PLANS

The IDEA requires school officials to conduct functional behavioral assessments (FBAs) and implement behavioral intervention services and modifications, commonly known as behavior intervention plans (BIPs), if they have not already done so, or to review such assessments and plans, if they have been implemented, whenever disciplinary consequences that may result in changes in placements may be imposed (20 U.S.C. §1415(k)(1)(D)(ii); 34 C.F.R. § 300.530(d)(1)(ii)). Even so, neither the IDEA nor its regulations provide much guidance as to what should be included in FBAs or BIPs. To date, there have been few judicial opinions or due process hearings dealing with the contents of either FBAs or BIPs.

The IDEA requires school officials to conduct FBAs and develop BIPs whenever they seek to remove students from their current placements and transfer them to interim alternative educational settings for up to 45 days, regardless of whether the students' behaviors are found to be manifestations of their disabilities. Further, FBAs and BIPs apply to situations where school officials seek to change students' placements for more than 10 school days when the misconduct is determined to be caused by their disabilities (20 U.S.C. § 1415(k)(1)(D); 34 C.F.R. § 300.530(d)).

> The IDEA requires school officials to conduct FBAs and develop BIPs whenever they seek to remove students from their current placements and transfer them to interim alternative educational settings for up to 45 days, regardless of whether the students' behaviors are found to be manifestations of their disabilities.

Another section of the IDEA requires educators to develop FBAs and BIPs if they were not already in place whenever school officials determine that students' misconduct was a manifestation of their disabilities and officials seek to change students' placements (20 U.S.C. § 1415(k)(1)(F)(i); 34 C.F.R. § 300.530(f)(1)(i)). In other words, FBAs and BIPs are pretty much required whenever school officials seek to impose suspensions of more than 10 days, expulsions, or transfers to interim alternative settings for up to 45 days.

FBAs should be completed prior to any manifestation determinations (*Coleman v. Newburgh Enlarged City School District*, 2004, 2007). In situations where BIPs were in place at the time of the disciplinary actions, they must be reviewed and modified, if necessary (20 U.S.C. § 1415(k)(1)(F)(ii); 34 C.F.R. § 300.530(f)(1)(ii)). Another section of the IDEA requires school officials to develop positive behavioral interventions, strategies, and supports to address behavior that impedes learning for students with disabilities or their classmates (20 U.S.C. § 1414(d)(3)(B)(i)).

As should all decisions that concern students' educational placements, FBAs and BIPs should be developed by IEP teams. Although it is not required, school personnel would be prudent to include the development of FBAs and BIPs as part of the annual IEP process for all students with disabilities who have a history of or potential for misbehavior. In fact, in one case, a federal trial court in Alabama labeled as flawed a school board's argument that a behavior plan was unwarranted because the behaviors in question were related to the student's disability (*Escambia County Board of Education v. Benton,* 2005). In keeping with the general requirements of the IDEA regarding assessments and IEPs, FBAs and BIPs should be individualized (*Mason City Community School District,* 2000).

As stated earlier, neither the IDEA nor its regulations specify what elements should be included in FBAs. However, at a minimum it would be prudent to include elements such as observations of the students that document aspects of, and the types of, their behaviors; analysis of the situations that trigger misbehaviors; analysis of the effectiveness of previous interventions; medical, psychological, and social factors that could impact student behavior; and any information that could provide insight into the students' behavior.

At the same time, the IDEA and its regulations provide little guidance as to what elements must be included in BIPs. As noted by the Seventh Circuit, insofar as neither the IDEA nor its regulations create any specific substantive requirements for BIPs, a school board's behavior plan could not have fallen short of substantive criteria that do not exist (*Alex R. v. Forrestville Valley Community Unit School District,* 2004). In the case that came before it, which originated in Illinois, parents had challenged the appropriateness of their son's overall IEP. The court held that as a matter of law the school board's BIP was not substantively invalid, since the IDEA had not established substantive requirements.

The federal trial court in Maine stated the obvious by indicating that behavior plans should encompass strategies for dealing with students' behavior (*Rome School Committee v. Mrs. B.,* 2000). Such an approach includes strategies for dealing with behaviors at the time they surface as well as long-term strategies for preventing future occurrences. The plans also should include supports that are to be provided for students to help them respond appropriately to the situations that tend to precipitate the behaviors. Finally, BIPs should outline expected behaviors, delineate inappropriate behaviors, and specify the positive and negative consequences for student behaviors.

In developing BIPs it is important to remember that the purpose of all discipline is to teach students appropriate behavior. To this end, BIPs should not be overly punitive. Rather, BIPs should include provisions that are clearly designed to assist students in developing more appropriate behaviors (*Goleta Union Elementary School District*, 1999). That is not to say that negative consequences cannot be included in BIPs, since both positive and negative consequences are normally part of most behavior improvement strategies. However, the focus of BIPs should be on teaching appropriate behavior instead of punishing misconduct.

The IDEA fails to specify whether BIPs should be part of students' IEPs or should be separate documents. In fact, as noted by the Eighth Circuit, the IDEA does not even require that BIPs be in writing (*School Board of Independent School District No. 11 v. Renollett*, 2006). The court was convinced that school officials in Minnesota met the IDEA's mandates by responding to a student's behavioral incidents with set procedures. Despite the IDEA's lack of a requirement for a written plan, it is always best to put BIPs in writing so that all concerned are clear about the procedures that should be implemented when needed. Given the fact that a BIP can play an integral part of any student's overall program, it makes sense to incorporate these plans as part of the IEPs by including them as addenda or attached documents.

BIPs are not required in all situations. For example, in a case from New Hampshire, the First Circuit agreed with an IEP team's decision that a student who had moderate mental retardation along with many other disabilities did not require a BIP to receive an appropriate education (*Lessard v. Wilton Lyndeborough Cooperative School District*, 2008). The court pointed out that BIPs are required only when certain disciplinary actions occur. This decision notwithstanding, if there is any question as to whether BIPs are required, prudent school administrators should err on the side of caution and develop such plans for students.

Once FBAs and BIPs are in place, they should be reviewed periodically (*Modesto City School District*, 1998). At a minimum, BIPs should be reviewed annually, along with students' IEPs. However, more frequent review, and revision, may well be warranted for students who face disciplinary actions, insofar as this would be an indication that existing FBAs and BIPs may be ineffective. The IDEA requires IEP teams to review, and modify, FBAs and BIPs if necessary whenever they determine that misconduct was a manifestation of students' disabilities (20 U.S.C. § 1415(k)(1)(F)(ii); 34 C.F.R. § 300.530(f)(1)(ii)).

EXPULSIONS OF STUDENTS WITH DISABILITIES

The IDEA, as amended, does not prohibit the expulsion of students with disabilities in all circumstances. When contemplating an expulsion,

> The IDEA, as amended, does not prohibit the expulsion of students with disabilities in all circumstances. When contemplating an expulsion, school personnel must first determine whether misconduct was a manifestation of a student's disabilities.

school personnel must first determine whether misconduct was a manifestation of a student's disabilities (20 U.S.C. § 1415(k)(E); 34 C.F.R. § 300.530(e)). This judgment must be made by a manifestation review committee, consisting of members of the school's IEP team in consort with the student's parents, along with other individuals who may have relevant information, within 10 school days of any decision to change the student's placement. If the review committee decides that the misconduct was a manifestation of the student's disabilities, then the student cannot be expelled. Even so, students may be transferred to more restrictive educational settings by following the IDEA's normal change in placement procedures. The IDEA requires school personnel to notify the parents of students with disabilities in writing prior to making planned changes in their placements (20 U.S.C. § 1415(b)(3)) and to afford them the opportunity to object to planned changes (20 U.S.C. § 1415(b)(6)).

If manifestation review committees determine that the misconduct in question was not a manifestation of the student's disabilities, then the student may be expelled. At this point, the student would be entitled to full expulsion hearings. When students are properly expelled by following the IDEA's procedures, the IDEA makes it clear that school boards still must provide special education services during the expulsion periods (20 U.S.C. § 1412(a)(1)(A)). This provision is in line with the position previously taken by the U.S. Department of Education (*Boggus Letter,* 1993; *Davis Letter,* 1989; *Hartman Letter,* 1995; *New Letter,* 1989; *Price Letter,* 1993; *Smith Letter,* 1992; *Symkowick Letter,* 1991; *Taylor Letter,* 1993; *Uhler Letter,* 1992) and effectively reverses the Fourth and Seventh Circuits' decisions in *Commonwealth of Virginia Department of Education v. Riley* (1997) and *Doe v. Board of Education of Oak Park & River Forest High School District 200* (1997) discussed in Chapter 3. This modification to the IDEA has ended the controversy that existed among the federal appellate circuits (Osborne, 1997). Subsequently, the federal trial court in Maine recognized that an IEP developed to cover an expulsion period for a student who was removed for a drug infraction did not need to embrace all of the subjects that he would have taken if he had remained enrolled in school (*Farrin v. Maine School Administrative District No. 59,* 2001). The court added that the IEP would have been sufficient as long as it still provided him with the opportunity to obtain the credits and skills he needed for graduation.

SUSPENSIONS OF STUDENTS WITH DISABILITIES

The IDEA affords school personnel the authority to suspend students with disabilities for not more than 10 school days by following the normal minimal due process procedures, as long as similar sanctions would be applied to students who do not have disabilities (20 U.S.C. § 1415(k)(1)(B); 34 C.F.R. § 300.530(b)). School officials must be cautious with multiple suspensions in a school year, since the IDEA's regulations stipulate that a series of removals that result in patterns of exclusions that cumulate to more than 10 school days may be considered changes in placement (34 C.F.R. § 300.536(a)). The length of each removal, the total amount of time the students are removed, and the proximity of exclusions to one another are all factors that should be considered in determining whether changes in placement have occurred. Where cumulative suspensions exceed 10 school days and may be considered patterns of exclusion, school officials must treat the situations as expulsions, meaning that manifestation review hearings must be conducted. As indicated above, officials must conduct FBAs if they have not already done so, and they must take action to address the students' misconduct for suspensions that caused them to be removed for more than 10 days in a school year (20 U.S.C. § 1415(k)(1)(D)(ii); 34 C.F.R. § 300.530(d)(1)(ii)).

> The IDEA affords school personnel the authority to suspend students with disabilities for not more than 10 school days by following the normal minimal due process procedures, as long as similar sanctions would be applied to students who do not have disabilities.

Even so, in a case from Minnesota, the Eighth Circuit did not fault school officials who repeatedly suspended a student for various acts of misconduct such as bringing a knife to school, fighting, and assaulting staff (*M. M. ex rel. L. R. v. Special School District No. 1,* 2008). After the child's mother rejected school officials' offers to transfer her daughter to a more appropriate setting or provide homebound instruction, the court was convinced that the board was not liable for continuing to impose suspensions, since the student was a danger to herself and others.

The IDEA clearly permits the emergency removal of dangerous students with disabilities, even when the misconduct stems from their disabilities (20 U.S.C. § 1415(k)(1)(B); 34 C.F.R. § 300.530(b)). Under the Supreme Court's ruling in *Honig v. Doe* (*Honig,* 1988), discussed in Chapter 3, an emergency removal may be accomplished by

> The IDEA clearly permits the emergency removal of dangerous students with disabilities, even when the misconduct stems from their disabilities.

following the normal *Goss v. Lopez* (*Goss,* 1975) due process procedures as outlined in Chapter 2. This means that students may be removed immediately and that due process hearings may take place later. However, hearings should take place as quickly as possible.

MANIFESTATION DETERMINATIONS

School officials must conduct manifestation determinations before making any decisions about whether to change the placements of students with disabilities who violate school rules (20 U.S.C. § 1415(k)(1)(E)(i); 34 C.F.R. § 300.530(e)(1)). Although originally this was required only by case law, the IDEA and its regulations now spell out the procedures for conducting manifestation determinations (20 U.S.C. § 1415(k)(1)(E); 34 C.F.R. § 300.530(e)).

The IDEA requires local school boards or other educational agencies and relevant members of IEP teams to conduct manifestation determinations in conjunction with students' parents (20 U.S.C. § 1415(k)(1)(E)(i); 34 C.F.R. § 300.530(e)(1)). This section of the IDEA further stipulates that in making the manifestation determinations, the review committees must consider all relevant information in students' files, including their IEPs, teacher observations, and relevant information provided by the parents. This does not mean, however, that every member of review committees must read every piece of information in the students' files before the hearings. The review of information may occur either before or during the course of the manifestation hearings (*Fitzgerald v. Fairfax County School Board,* 2008).

In deciding whether misconduct is a manifestation of a student's disability, review committees are required to consider "if the conduct in question was caused by, or had a direct and substantial relationship to, the child's disability" (20 U.S.C. § 1415(k)(1)(E)(i)(I)) or "if the conduct in question was the direct result of the local educational agency's failure to implement the IEP" (20 U.S.C. § 1415(k)(1)(E)(i)(II)). The federal trial court in Maine affirmed a manifestation review committee's finding that a student's misconduct was not a manifestation of his disability for a student with a learning disability who was expelled for selling marijuana in school. The court noted that the student understood school rules, and there was evidence that his actions, which took place over several hours, were not impulsive (*Farrin v. Maine School Administrative District No. 59,* 2001). Similarly, a federal trial court in Virginia was convinced that misconduct was not a manifestation

> In deciding whether misconduct is a manifestation of a student's disability, review committees are required to consider "if the conduct in question was caused by, or had a direct and substantial relationship to, the child's disability" or "if the conduct in question was the direct result of the local educational agency's failure to implement the IEP."

of a student's disability in a situation where the student, who was diagnosed as having an emotional disability, repeatedly shot paintballs at a school and school property over a period of several hours (*Fitzgerald v. Fairfax County School Board*, 2008). Evidence, albeit disputed by the student's parents, indicated that the student had planned the activity and enlisted peers to participate.

If manifestation review committees determine that misconduct was not a manifestation of students' disabilities, the students may be disciplined in the same manner as peers who do not have disabilities except that officials may not terminate the delivery of a free appropriate public education (FAPE) (20 U.S.C. § 1415(k)(1)(C); 34 C.F.R. § 300.530(c); 20 U.S.C. § 1412(a)(1)(A); 34 C.F.R. § 300.530(b)(2)). If the students' parents disagree with the teams' manifestation determinations, then they may request expedited hearings (20 U.S.C. § 1415(k)(3); 34 C.F.R. § 300.532).

Interestingly, although the IDEA requires manifestation review committees to consider whether any conduct in question was the direct result of school boards' failures to implement students' IEPs, it no longer requires evaluations regarding the appropriateness of the IEPs in the first place. Yet, given the IDEA's primary mandate that school boards must provide students with disabilities with a FAPE, the importance of having an appropriate IEP in place cannot be overemphasized. School officials would be hard pressed to defend a decision that misconduct was not a manifestation of students' disabilities when parents could demonstrate that the IEPs in place when the misconduct arose were not appropriate in the first place.

Definition of Manifestation

The IDEA's definition of the term *manifestation* is, unfortunately, general and vague. Other than using language stipulating that the misbehavior must be caused by or directly and substantially related to the students' disabilities or the direct result of school boards' failures to properly implement IEPs, the IDEA does not provide manifestation review committees with much guidance on making manifestation determinations.

A decision that was handed down before the current version of the IDEA was passed provides some guidance. Using language that comports with that in the current IDEA, the Ninth Circuit, in a case from California, declared that the relationship between the disabilities and the misconduct must be direct and causal (*Doe v.*

> Other than using language stipulating that the misbehavior must be caused by or directly and substantially related to the students' disabilities or the direct result of school boards' failures to properly implement IEPs, the IDEA does not provide manifestation review committees with much guidance on making manifestation determinations.

Maher, 1986). In a footnote, the court wrote that the term refers to "conduct that is caused by, or has a direct and substantial relationship" to the students' disabilities (p. 1480, n. 8). The court further explained that the students' disabilities must significantly impair their behavioral controls. The court added that the term does not embrace conduct that "bears only an attenuated relationship" to the disabilities.

When the Supreme Court reviewed the Ninth Circuit's decision, under the name *Honig v. Doe* (1988), regrettably, it did not provide a definition of manifestation. While the students in *Honig* were classified as emotionally disturbed, the issue of whether their infractions were manifestations of their disabilities was not before the Court. Although there is no definitive Supreme Court pronouncement regarding the definition of the term *manifestation,* recent lower court decisions provide some guidance. Insofar as state special education laws may provide more direction, educators should take them into consideration.

As one court noted, whether students have the ability to understand school rules is an important issue. The federal trial court in Maine supported a school board's analysis that selling marijuana in school was not a manifestation of a learning disabled student's disability (*Farrin v. Maine School Administrative District No. 59,* 2001). The facts revealed that the student's IEP did not address discipline except to stipulate that he would be subject to regular disciplinary consequences. The court was convinced that the student understood school rules and that his actions, which took place over several hours, were not impulsive. As indicated by the Maine court as well as a federal trial court in Virginia (*Fitzgerald v. Fairfax County School Board,* 2008), the facts that misbehavior was preplanned and took place over several hours, and thus was not an impulsive act, can be a critical consideration.

Another factor is whether students understood the consequences of their misbehaviors. In a case from Virginia, the Fourth Circuit affirmed that the actions of a student who was classified as emotionally disturbed were not a manifestation of his disability (*A. W. ex rel. Wilson v. Fairfax County School Board,* 2004). The student was suspended, and officials initiated expulsion proceedings, after he persuaded another student to put a threatening note in the computer file of a third student. The manifestation review committee decided that the student's IEP adequately compensated for his emotional disability and that his disability did not prevent him from understanding that his actions violated school rules. Further, the Fourth Circuit did not find anything in the student's IEP or the school psychologist's evaluation report to suggest that his interpersonal difficulties were so substantial that they could not be managed by outside counseling or that they would be exacerbated by placement in the general curriculum with other students. The court ascertained that the student was aware of the consequences of sending the threatening note and even anticipated them when he enlisted a peer to place the note. In light of the circumstances of the student's misconduct having demonstrated forethought and investigation, the court reasoned that it was not a manifestation of his disability.

A judgment by a federal trial court in New York demonstrates that misconduct that may be in response to the actions of others could be related to a disability (*Coleman v. Newburgh Enlarged City School District,* 2004, 2007). A special education student was removed from the general education program following an altercation with a peer. Following a manifestation determination, the manifestation review committee decided that the student had the ability to control his behavior and that his misconduct was not a manifestation of his disability. The court was convinced that the manifestation determination was incorrect, insofar as the student claimed that his actions were in response to taunting from the other child about the fact that he received special education services. The court acknowledged that the student's disability was thus directly involved in the altercation.

Making Manifestation Determinations

The IDEA stipulates that manifestation determinations are to be made by relevant members of the schools' IEP teams and the parents along with officials from local educational agencies (LEAs) or school boards. This approach permits school administrators who were not part of the original IEP teams, as LEA representatives, to participate in making manifestation determinations. For example, an administrator who investigated an incident of misconduct but was not part of the offending student's IEP team could be a member of the manifestation review committee because that person would be relevant to the purpose of the determination. As shown by a case from Virginia, the IDEA's provision that the manifestation is to be conducted by members of the IEP team as determined by the parent and the LEA does not mean that the parents and school officials must agree on the composition of the review committee (*Fitzgerald v. Fairfax County School Board,* 2008). The parents may invite individuals to the hearing but do not have the right to veto members selected by the school board. Further, according to the Virginia court, not all members of the manifestation review committee need to know the student personally.

As with all placement decisions under the IDEA, manifestation determinations must be individualized and may not be made on the basis of characteristics generally exhibited by others with the same disabilities (*J. B. by N. K. v. Independent School District No. 191, Burnsville, Minnesota,* 1995). In this respect, manifestation review committees must consider whether disabilities, as they affect individual students, caused the specific misconduct.

An important consideration would be the severity of the student's disability (*Elk Grove Unified School District*, 1989). Review committees should also consider whether students subject to manifestation determinations have any previously unidentified disabilities that might have caused their misconduct (*Modesto City Schools*, 1994). Further, manifestation determinations must be grounded in specific incidents. Again, generalizations cannot be the determinative factor. Instead, review committees must consider whether the disabilities, as exhibited by individual students, could have caused the misconduct that gave rise to the disciplinary action.

The IDEA requires manifestation review committees to consider students' IEPs, staff observations of students, information in students' files, and other relevant information provided by the parents (20 U.S.C. § 1415(k)(1)(E)(i); 34 C.F.R. § 300.530(e)(1)). Review committees should also include evaluation and diagnostic data in the files that they review. When evaluation data are not current for students, it is best to conduct reevaluations (*In re Child With Disabilities*, 1989; *Sioux City (IA) School District*, 1989). Even though the IDEA requires reevaluations only every three years at a minimum (unless the parent and the local educational agency agree that a reevaluation is unnecessary), one is justified whenever it is warranted to meet students' needs (20 U.S.C. § 1414(a)(2)). Thus, more frequent reevaluations may sometimes be required. A sudden change in students' behavior is one such circumstance that could merit a reevaluation (*In re Doe*, 2002).

> The IDEA requires manifestation review committees to consider students' IEPs, staff observations of students, information in students' files, and other relevant information provided by the parents.

At least one court has decreed that a reevaluation is required whenever a significant change in placement is being considered (*Brimmer v. Traverse City Area Public Schools*, 1994). In addition, the federal Office for Civil Rights (OCR) stated that under Section 504 of the Rehabilitation Act (Rehabilitation Act, Section 504, 2006), IEP teams must conduct reevaluations before significant changes in placement may occur (*OCR Memorandum: Long-term Suspension or Expulsion of Handicapped Students*, 1988). Reevaluations should include psychological assessments designed specifically to elicit data relative to the behavior that brought about the disciplinary actions (*OCR Memorandum: Suspensions of Handicapped Students—Deciding Whether Misbehavior Is Caused By a Child's Handicapping Condition*, 1989). If those who conducted the most recent assessments are not part of the review committees making the manifestation determination, they should be consulted regarding the specific incidents in question.

Other factors that could have caused the misbehavior may be considered (*Elk Grove Unified School District*, 1989). However, when several factors contribute to the misbehavior and the students' disabilities are just one of the contributing factors, the connection between disability and misconduct has been established. If the manifestation review committees determine that misconduct was a manifestation of students' disabilities, because the causal connection has been made or results from a failure to implement the students' IEPs, students may not be suspended for more than 10 days (*Uhler Letter*, 1992), but school officials should reconsider the students' placements (*Boggus Letter*, 1993). Nonpunitive changes in placements may be appropriate and should be implemented subject to applicable procedural safeguards and the IDEA's least restrictive environment provision. Students may be suspended for more than 10 days if their disabilities or educators' failure to implement IEPs properly did not cause the misconduct.

One question that has arisen since the latest IDEA amendments went into effect is whether manifestations are established when it can be shown that students' IEPs or placements were not appropriate in the first place. Prior to the adoption of the 2004 amendments to the IDEA, the law did include a notation that inappropriate IEPs or placements could be factors that establish a manifestation (Russo, Osborne, & Borreca, 2006). However, the latest version of the IDEA does not require manifestation review committees to consider the appropriateness of IEPs and placements when making manifestation determinations. Still, the IDEA does indicate that a nexus is established if students' misconduct was caused by the failure to implement IEPs. It seems ironic that a failure to implement an IEP establishes a manifestation, but a failure to develop an appropriate IEP and placement in the first place does not do so. In either case, students are deprived of the FAPE to which they are entitled under the IDEA due to school boards' failures to carry out the IDEA's mandates. It remains to be seen how courts will interpret the IDEA in light of the new language. In this respect, courts may consider school boards' failures to provide FAPEs to be contributing factors in students' misbehavior. Insofar as the overall intent of the IDEA is to provide a FAPE, it is unlikely that courts would support expulsions after finding that the misconduct was caused by school boards' failures to adhere to the law's basic requirements.

> One question that has arisen since the latest IDEA amendments went into effect is whether manifestations are established when it can be shown that students' IEPs or placements were not appropriate in the first place.

OCR has provided guidelines for making manifestation determinations under the provisions of Section 504. Although many of the OCR guidelines are identical to the standards under the IDEA, they are repeated here for clarity. According to OCR, reevaluations that include determinations of whether misconduct was caused by students' disabilities are required before significant changes in placement may occur (*OCR Memorandum*, 1988). These determinations must be made by groups including individuals personally familiar with the students and who have knowledge about special education (*OCR Memorandum*, 1989). These groups should consider psychological evaluation data related to behavior and other information that is recent enough to afford an understanding of the students' current behavior when making their judgment. If educators, in conjunction with parents, decide thatthe students' misconduct was caused by their disabilities, then they must address the appropriateness of the students' current educational placements (*OCR Memorandum*, 1988). If placements are inappropriate, then IEP teams must take steps to place the students in appropriate settings.

In sum, at least some individuals on committees that make manifestation determinations should have personal knowledge of the students and their disabilities. Manifestation determinations must be individualized and incident specific. Unless the latest evaluation data are fairly recent, reevaluations, including psychological and behavioral assessments, should be conducted as part of the determinations. Evaluation data should also include observations of the students in their educational environments. While each determination must be individualized and conducted in light of students' unique situations, it is difficult to provide further guidelines. Even so, the next section seeks to provide such guidelines.

Manifestation Decision-Making Guidelines

Little case law has emerged regarding manifestation determinations since the 1997 and 2004 amendments to the IDEA became law. Even so, much of the pre-1997 case law can still provide some guidance to assist school officials with the difficult, and challenging, task of evaluating whether specific acts of misconduct are manifestations of students' disabilities.

The suggestions that follow are based on that case law. School officials are cautioned, however, that above all else, all manifestation determinations must be individualized. Thus, the suggestions here may need to be adjusted to fit the individual needs of students and situations.

> To the extent possible, manifestation determinations should be made by the same individuals who were involved in conducting the students' most recent evaluations and developing their last IEPs, since these are likely the professionals who would best know the students.

To the extent possible, manifestation determinations should be made by the same individuals who were involved in conducting the students' most recent evaluations and developing their last IEPs, since these are likely the professionals who would best know the students. Even so, IEP team membership is not static, and at different times different individuals may fill the statutory roles (*Fitzgerald v. Fairfax County School Board*, 2008). Additional persons may be added to manifestation review committees if needed. For example, school personnel who witnessed the misconduct and could provide detailed descriptions of the incidents could provide insight into the cause(s) of the misbehavior. Also, teachers who were not part of the students' IEP teams but who know the students well could offer valuable assistance and insights. If available evaluation data are more than one year old, at least partial reevaluations to update critical assessments should be conducted before manifestation decisions are undertaken.

Once assembled, the committees who are to make manifestation determinations should carefully examine and consider the following factors:

• *The students' disability classifications.* Identification and classification of students as emotionally disturbed, behaviorally disordered, or something comparable may provide support for the position that acts of misconduct are a manifestation of the students' disabilities. Still, manifestation determinations cannot be made on the basis of the students' disability classifications alone. The fact that students are classified as emotionally disturbed or behaviorally disordered does not mean that they are unable to understand the impact and consequences of misbehaviors or are unable to control behaviors. By the same token, the fact that students have not been categorized as emotionally disturbed or behaviorally disordered does not mean that their misconduct is unrelated to their disabilities. Judgments must be made as to whether the students' disabilities either prevented them from understanding the consequences of their behavior or impaired their ability to control offending behavior.

• *The students' IEPs.* Information in the students' IEPs may provide some evidence as to whether the students' disabilities may have caused them to misbehave. For example, comments that students suffer from poor self-esteem, do not understand cause-and-effect relationships, act impulsively, or have low frustration tolerance could imply that under certain circumstances, their misconduct could be related to their disabilities. Naturally, a direct statement such as, "The student has difficulty following school rules" would provide a convincing indication of a causal connection.

• *Anecdotal teacher notes.* Anecdotal notes made by teachers as either report card comments or notations in school records often provide insight into students' past behavior. In addition to providing a record of past behavior, these notes may supply specific information about the nature of past misconduct and the context in which those behaviors occurred.

• *Recent evaluation data.* Evaluation data, particularly psychological data, may be most beneficial in making manifestation determinations. If the evaluation data indicate that students have an inclination to be disruptive, become easily angered, or may lash out when feeling threatened, misconduct can be predicted. Further, evaluation data may provide information that students have poor impulse control, do not fully understand the consequences of their behavior, or do not know right from wrong. This information can provide valuable clues as to whether there is a relationship between the students' disabilities and misconduct. Evaluation data should be current enough that they relate to the students' present situations. FBAs should be completed if they are not current. FBAs on file should be reviewed to make sure that they are accurate and up-to-date. Observations of the students in the environment in which the misbehavior occurred would provide context-specific information and should be part of this process.

- *The students' behavioral history.* An important question that manifestation review committees must consider is whether students' current misconduct is part of a pattern of misbehavior or an isolated incident. An act of misconduct that is part of a pattern is more likely to be an indication of disability-related behavior than a single isolated incident.

- *The incident situation.* Students behave differently in different situations. An analysis of the specific situations that led to acts of misconduct may provide understanding about possible relationships between the misconduct and the students' disabilities. Manifestation review committees should consider how the students' disabilities affected their judgment in the incident situations or interpretation of the events that led to the misbehaviors. The review committees must also address whether students understood and were aware of the consequences of their misconduct.

After manifestation review committees examine all pertinent information and consider the above factors, they should proceed as they would in making any other decisions regarding students' identifications, classifications, or placements. In this respect, there is no substitute for sound professional judgment. There are no cookbook procedures for determining whether the information available shows that the misconduct was a manifestation of the students' disabilities. Hence, in making their decisions, personnel must rely on their professional knowledge, their knowledge of the students, and their understanding of the circumstances that led to the misconduct. The IDEA does not require review committees to reach a consensus regarding their final determinations. In fact, parent members of review committees may sometimes disagree with school personnel regarding the final outcome. The IDEA's emphasis on parental involvement does not give the parents the right to veto any decisions made by the other members of the review committee (*Fitzgerald v. Fairfax County School Board*, 2008). If parents do disagree, they may file an appeal as outlined in the next section.

HEARINGS TO CHALLENGE
MANIFESTATION DETERMINATIONS

As are any matters related to students' special education programs, manifestation determinations are subject to the IDEA's administrative appeals process. The IDEA affords parents the right to request hearings if they disagree with those decisions (20 U.S.C. § 1415(k)(3); 34 C.F.R. § 300.532). If parents choose to contest manifestation determinations and their children have been removed from the educational settings they were in when the offending behavior occurred, then the students remain in the alternative placements until the appeals are resolved (20 U.S.C. § 1415(k)(4)(A); 34 C.F.R. § 300.533). These hearings must be expedited, meaning that they must take place within 20 school days of the requests for hearings and decisions must be made within 10 school days of the hearings (20 U.S.C. § 1415(k)(4); 34 C.F.R. § 300.532(c)). Even so, any long-term suspensions or expulsions could be stayed until the expedited hearings are concluded (*Boggus Letter,* 1993).

> As are any matters related to students' special education programs, manifestation determinations are subject to the IDEA's administrative appeals process.

Parents have the right to appeal any administrative hearing decisions to federal or state courts (20 U.S.C. § 1415(i)(2)). The parental right to appeal includes adjudications rendered by hearing officers regarding contested manifestation determinations. Again, the students remain in their alternative placements until all appeals have been completed. In fact, in one case, the Second Circuit ruled that a federal trial court from New York improperly issued an injunction reinstating a student to his former placement while appeals were still pending, even though the lower court had found that the school's determination of no manifestation was incorrect (*Coleman v. Newburgh Enlarged City School District,* 2007). The court was of the opinion that even though the student had a right not to be removed from school based on an erroneous determination of no manifestation, he lacked the right to reinstatement while the determination was being reviewed.

Although parents are entitled to expedited hearings when they challenge school board decisions regarding the discipline of their children, they may not proceed directly to court. For example, a federal trial court in Virginia upheld the IDEA's stipulation that parents must exhaust administrative remedies prior to filing a lawsuit even when challenging a manifestation determination (*A. W. ex rel. Wilson v. Fairfax County School Board,* 2008). Similarly, a federal trial court in New Jersey required parents to first exhaust their administrative remedies when raising a claim that the school board failed to conduct a manifestation review hearing (*M. G. v. Crisfield*, 2008).

Some frequently asked questions about suspensions and expulsions of students with disabilities are summarized in Figure 4.1.

Figure 4.1   Frequently Asked Questions

Q. When should school officials complete functional behavioral assessments and develop behavior intervention plans?

A. Functional behavioral assessments (FBAs) should be completed whenever school officials contemplate removing special education students from their current educational settings for more than 10 school days for disciplinary reasons. Thus, FBAs should be conducted whenever school officials contemplate suspensions that cumulate to more than 10 days, expulsions, or transfers to alternate educational settings for up to 45 days. Further, whenever educators determined that misconduct was a manifestation of students' disabilities, they should complete FBAs and develop BIPs to prevent the misbehaviors from continuing.

Q. To what extent may students with disabilities be suspended?

A. Students with disabilities may be suspended for up to 10 consecutive school days to the same extent that students who do not have disabilities would be suspended for similar rule infractions. For suspensions of 10 days or less, school disciplinarians may follow normal suspension procedures.

Q. May students with disabilities be given multiple suspensions?

A. School officials must exercise caution when administering multiple suspensions that cumulatively exceed 10 days in a school year, as any series of removals that result in a pattern of exclusion may be considered changes in placement. Officials must consider the total number of days of exclusion, the length of each suspension, and the proximity of suspensions to one another. To this end, school officials need to be careful whenever the cumulative days of suspensions in a school year exceeds 10, especially if the suspensions were close together. Further, multiple suspensions for similar offenses without other interventions can be problematic.

Q. Under what circumstances may students with disabilities be expelled?

A. Students with disabilities may be expelled only if manifestation review committees determined that their misbehavior was not a manifestation of their disabilities.

Q. The IDEA stipulates that students with disabilities must continue to receive special education services even if they have been expelled. Doesn't this in effect nullify an expulsion?

A. Students with disabilities must continue to receive their special education services during an expulsion period. Even so, these students still may be removed from general education settings. School boards may provide special education services in a variety of other settings such as segregated special education classes, alternative schools, special education day and residential schools, or via homebound instruction. Thus, although the students continue to receive the special education services to which they are entitled under the IDEA, they may be removed from the general education environments and may be given those services in restrictive placements away from their classmates.

SUMMARY

The IDEA provides students with disabilities with additional procedural protections when faced with disciplinary sanctions. Still, the IDEA does not prevent school officials from taking disciplinary actions. Students with disabilities may be suspended for periods of up to 10 school days as long as similar consequences would be imposed on students who are not disabled. Students with disabilities may also be expelled if their misconduct was not a manifestation of their disabilities. If the misbehavior was a manifestation of the students' disabilities, they may not be expelled but may be transferred to more restrictive placements as long as officials follow the IDEA's change in placement procedures.

In evaluating whether misconduct is a manifestation of a student's disabilities, school officials, in conjunction with the student's parents, must consider whether the misbehavior was caused by or had a direct and substantial relationship to the student's disabilities. Further, teams must find a manifestation if the transgression was caused by the student's IEP being improperly implemented. Moreover, teams must render manifestation determinations whenever school officials contemplate removing students with disabilities from their educational settings for more than 10 school days.

The IDEA requires school officials to conduct functional behavioral assessments and implement behavior intervention plans under specified circumstances. School officials should complete FBAs whenever they contemplate removing special education students from their current educational settings for more than 10 school days for disciplinary reasons. Additionally, whenever it has been determined that misconduct was a manifestation of students' disabilities, teams should complete FBAs and develop BIPs to prevent the misbehaviors from continuing.

RECOMMENDATIONS FOR PRACTITIONERS

- Make case-by-case determinations of the disciplinary action to be taken whenever unique circumstances exist.
- Conduct FBAs and develop BIPs whenever suspensions of more than 10 days, expulsions, or transfers to interim alternative settings for up to 45 days are contemplated.
- Review any BIPs that were in place when the misconduct occurred to make sure that they are current and appropriate.
- Include the development of FBAs and BIPs as part of the annual IEP process for all students with disabilities who have a history of or potential for misbehavior.

- Conduct a manifestation review whenever a suspension of more than 10 school days or an expulsion is contemplated by following the procedures outlined in the IDEA.
- In conducting a manifestation review, assemble as many members of the original IEP team as possible, and invite other relevant school personnel to participate. Allow parents to also invite additional individuals to participate if they desire.
- Consider all relevant information in a student's file along with new information at a manifestation review hearing. If possible, to save time and make sure that all members are familiar with this information, provide as much information as possible beforehand.
- Fully consider all information provided by parents at a manifestation review.
- If students are expelled, after all IDEA procedures have been followed, continue to provide special education services.
- When suspending students with disabilities, be sure that the same sanction would be applied to their peers without disabilities for similar infractions.
- Avoid serial suspensions that result in a pattern of exclusion.
- Check state laws and regulations to see if any additional restrictions are placed on suspension.
- Provide parents with an expedited hearing if they disagree with the manifestation determination.
- As with all matters relating to the education of students with disabilities, maintain strict confidentiality.

WHAT'S NEXT

Suspensions and expulsions are not the only disciplinary sanctions available to school officials. Students with disabilities also may be transferred to other, possibly more restrictive, programs or to interim alternative educational settings for disciplinary reasons. The next chapter presents information on these and other options.

REFERENCES

A. W. ex rel. Wilson v. Fairfax County School Board, 372 F.3d 674 (4th Cir. 2004).
A. W. ex rel. Wilson v. Fairfax County School Board, 548 F. Supp.2d 219 (E.D. Va. 2008).
Alex R. v. Forrestville Valley Community Unit School District, 375 F.3d 603 (7th Cir. 2004).
Boggus Letter, 20 IDELR 625 (OSEP 1993).
Brimmer v. Traverse City Area Public Schools, 872 F. Supp. 447 (W.D. Mich. 1994).

Child With Disabilities, In re, 16 EHLR 207 (SEA Cal. 1989).

Code of Federal Regulations (C.F.R.), as cited.

Coleman v. Newburgh Enlarged City School District, 319 F. Supp.2d 446 (S.D. N.Y. 2004), *vacated and reversed on other grounds,* 503 F.3d 198 (2d Cir. 2007).

Commonwealth of Virginia Department of Education v. Riley, 106 F.3d 559 (4th Cir. 1997).

Davis Letter, 16 EHLR 734 (OSERS 1989).

Doe, In re, 753 N.Y.S.2d 656 (N.Y. Fam. Ct. 2002).

Doe v. Board of Education of Oak Park & River Forest High School District 200, 115 F.3d 1273 (7th Cir. 1997).

Doe v. Maher, 793 F.2d 1470 (9th Cir. 1986), *affirmed on other grounds sub nom. Honig v. Doe,* 484 U.S. 305 (1988).

Elk Grove Unified School District, 16 EHLR 622 (SEA Cal. 1989).

Escambia County Board of Education v. Benton (S.D. Ala. 2005).

Farrin v. Maine School Administrative District No. 59, 165 F. Supp.2d 37 (D. Me. 2001).

Fitzgerald v. Fairfax County School Board, 556 F. Supp.2d 543 (E.D. Va. 2008).

Goleta Union Elementary School District, 31 IDELR 231 (SEA Cal. 1999).

Goss v. Lopez, 419 U.S. 565 (1975).

Hartman Letter, 23 IDELR 894 (OSEP 1995).

Honig v. Doe, 484 U.S. 305 (1988).

Individuals with Disabilities Education Act (IDEA), 20 U.S.C. §§ 1400–1482 (2006).

J. B. by N. K. v. Independent School District No. 191, Burnsville, Minnesota, 21 IDELR 1157 (D. Minn. 1995).

Lessard v. Wilton Lyndeborough Cooperative School District, 518 F.3d 18 (1st Cir. 2008).

M. G. v. Crisfield, 547 F. Supp.2d 399 (D.N.J. 2008).

M. M. ex rel. L. R. v. Special School District No. 1, 512 F.3d 455 (8th Cir. 2008).

Mason City Community School District, 32 IDELR 216 (SEA Iowa 2000).

Modesto City School District, 30 IDELR 179 (SEA Cal. 1998).

Modesto City Schools, 21 IDELR 685 (SEA Cal. 1994).

New Letter, EHLR 213:258 (OSERS 1989).

OCR memorandum: Long-term suspension or expulsion of handicapped students, EHLR 307:05 (OCR 1988).

OCR memorandum: Suspensions of handicapped students—deciding whether misbehavior is caused by a child's handicapping condition, 16 EHLR 491 (OCR 1989).

Osborne, A. G. (1997). Provision of special education services during an expulsion: *Commonwealth of Virginia v. Riley. Education Law Reporter, 118,* 557–569.

Price Letter, 20 IDELR 1256 (OSERS 1993).

Rehabilitation Act, Section 504, 29 U.S.C. § 794 (2006).

Rome School Committee v. Mrs. B., 2000 WL 762027 (D. Me. 2000).

Russo, C. J., Osborne, A. G., & Borreca, E. A. (2006). *What's changed? A side-by-side analysis of the 2006 and 1999 IDEA Part B regulations.* Horsham, PA: LRP.

School Board of Independent School District No. 11 v. Renollett, 440 F.3d 1007 (8th Cir. 2006).

Sioux City (IA) School District, 16 EHLR 308 (OCR 1989).

Smith Letter, 18 IDELR 685 (OSERS 1992).

Symkowick Letter, 17 EHLR 469 (OSERS 1991).

Taylor Letter, 20 IDELR 542 (OSERS 1993).

Uhler Letter, 18 IDELR 1238 (OSEP 1992).

United States Code (U.S.C.), as cited.

5 Transfers to More Restrictive Settings

Key Concepts in This Chapter

♦ Changes in Placement to More Restrictive Environments

♦ Transfers to Interim Alternative Placements for Weapon or Drug Violations or Infliction of Serious Bodily Injuries

♦ Injunctions to Remove Dangerous or Disruptive Students

INTRODUCTION

According to the U.S. Supreme Court's ruling in *Honig v. Doe* (*Honig*, 1988), school officials may immediately suspend students with disabilities for serious acts of misbehavior. While students are suspended, the Court anticipated that school officials and parents would work together to decide where students with disabilities would be placed following their suspensions. For the most part, the options would be either to return students to their former placements; develop new IEPs that would place them in other, possibly more restrictive, programs; transfer them to interim alternate placements for up to 45 days; or expel the students in cases where officials would have imposed similar penalties on students who did not have disabilities. The options that educators and parents select depend, of course, on the severity of the infractions and the likelihood that the students would continue to be discipline problems or the chance that they could continue to engage in behavior that would be dangerous to themselves or others.

As evidenced by the thousands of due process and judicial hearings that have occurred since the Individuals with Disabilities Education Act (IDEA, 2006) was initially passed in 1975, parents and school officials do not always agree on what is in the best interest of students. To this end, the IDEA and its regulations have established procedures so that school administrators can take the necessary steps to remove students who truly present a danger or potential for seriously disrupting the educational environment, even over the objections of their parents.

This chapter reviews the procedures and requirements that school officials must follow when they seek to transfer students with disabilities to other more restrictive placements. The chapter includes a discussion of the circumstances under which educators may transfer students to interim alternative educational settings for possession of weapons, knowing possession of drugs, or inflicting serious bodily injuries on others in schools or at school activities. In addition, the chapter provides information on the circumstances in which courts and hearing officers may issue injunctions to remove dangerous students with disabilities from the general education environment.

CHANGES IN PLACEMENT TO MORE RESTRICTIVE ENVIRONMENTS

Individualized education program (IEP) teams sometimes change the placements of students with disabilities. Teams often make such changes when they determine that the students' current educational placements are failing to meet their needs. The IDEA has established specific procedures for changing students' placements that must be followed regardless of the reasons for proposed changes.

When students with disabilities frequently commit disciplinary infractions, it may be an indication that their current placements are not appropriate. In such situations, school personnel should seek to place students in more appropriate educational settings even if the alternative settings are more restrictive. Educators may wish to transfer students with disabilities to more restrictive settings if IEP teams agree that students' misconduct was a manifestation of their disabilities and an expulsion is not an option. As indicated above, in *Honig* the Supreme Court suggested that school officials could use a 10-day suspension period to work out arrangements with parents for alternative placements when this occurs.

> When students with disabilities frequently commit disciplinary infractions, it may be an indication that their current placements are not appropriate. In such situations, school personnel should seek to place students in more appropriate educational settings even if the alternative settings are more restrictive.

Prior to making any permanent changes in students' placement to settings that are more restrictive, school officials must provide children and their parents with the IDEA's usual due process safeguards (*Boggus Letter*, 1993; *Jonathan G. v. Caddo Parish School Board*, 1994). At a minimum, school officials should provide parents with prior notice of their intent to make the changes in placements and afford them the opportunity to object (20 U.S.C. § (b)(3), (6)). In addition to the IDEA's change in placement procedures, regulations implementing Section 504 of the Rehabilitation Act (Rehabilitation Act, Section 504, 2006) require educators to conduct reevaluations prior to making significant changes in placement (34 C.F.R. § 104.35(a); *OCR Memorandum*, 1989).

If parents are aware of school officials' intent to change the placement and are opposed, they may object to proposed reevaluations. However, courts have issued orders allowing school personnel to reevaluate students over their parents' objections (*Andress v. Cleveland Independent School District*, 1995; *School Board of the County of Prince William v. Wills*, 1989; *School Board of the County of Stafford v. Farley*, 1990). If the parents disagree with the recommended changes in placement, they may contest them via due process hearings (20 U.S.C. § 1415(f); 20 U.S.C. § 1415(k)(3); 34 C.F.R. § 300.532). The hearing process normally can be lengthy, but due to the emergency nature of hearings that are requested as a result of proposed changes in placement for disciplinary reasons, the IDEA includes provisions for an expedited review that should take place within 20 days, with a decision issued within another 10 days (20 U.S.C. § 1415(k)(4)(B); 34 C.F.R. § 300.532(c)).

The IDEA provides alternatives to administrative hearings for dispute resolution over proposed placements for students with disabilities (Osborne & Russo, 2007). Specifically, the IDEA requires states, and consequently local school boards, to establish procedures for resolution meetings (20 U.S.C. § 1415(f)(1)(B)(i)) and mediation (20 U.S.C. § 1415(e)) when the parties have initiated requests for due process hearings. Again, in disputes over placements that are proposed for disciplinary reasons, the IDEA's regulations provide for an expedited process. Resolution sessions must occur within 7 days of receipt of requests for due process hearings unless the parties agree to use the mediation process. In any event, hearings may proceed if the parties fail to reach agreement within 15 days (34 C.F.R. § 300.532(c)(3)).

TRANSFERS TO INTERIM ALTERNATIVE PLACEMENTS FOR WEAPON OR DRUG VIOLATIONS OR INFLICTION OF SERIOUS BODILY INJURIES

Under the IDEA, school officials have the explicit authority to transfer students with disabilities to appropriate interim alternative educational settings for up to 45 school days. Educators may make such a change regardless of whether the behavior was a manifestation of the students' disabilities for any of the following infractions:

1. Carries or possesses a weapon to or at school, on school premises, or to or at a school function under the jurisdiction of a State or local educational agency;

2. Knowingly possesses or uses illegal drugs, or sells or solicits the sale of a controlled substance, while at school, on school premises, or at a school function under the jurisdiction of a State or local educational agency; or

3. Has inflicted serious bodily injury upon another person while at school, on school premises, or at a school function under the jurisdiction of a State or local educational agency. (20 U.S.C. § 1415(k)(1)(G))

These alternative placements must be in settings that allow students to progress in the general education curriculum and in which they continue to receive their special education services (20 U.S.C. § 1415(k)(1)(D)(i); 34 C.F.R. § 300.530(d)(1)(i)). IEP teams have been vested with the authority to select interim alternative educational settings (20 U.S.C. 1415(k)(2); 34 C.F.R. § 531). Further, officials must complete functional behavioral assessments (FBAs) and create behavior intervention plans (BIPs) that are designed to address the rule infractions so that the behavior does not recur (20 U.S.C. § 1415(k)(1)(D)(ii); 34 C.F.R. § 300.530(d)(1)(ii)). If FBAs or BIPs exist, they must be reviewed and modified, if necessary, to address the specific behaviors that resulted in the alternative placements. The requirements for conducting FBAs and developing BIPs were discussed earlier in Chapter 4.

This provision on interim alternative placements expanded the authority available to school officials under the Gun-Free School Zones Act of 1990 (2006). School officials may now exclude students with disabilities from inclusive settings due to drug violations or the infliction of serious bodily injuries in addition to weapons violations. The IDEA and its regulations define the terms *weapons, illegal drugs,* and *serious bodily injury* by reference to other federal legislation (20 U.S.C. § 1415(k)(7); 34 C.F.R. § 300.530(i)).

The IDEA's definition of a dangerous weapon is an expansion of the one that was contained in the Gun-Free Schools Act. The current definition of a dangerous weapon includes, in addition to firearms, other instruments, devices, materials, and substances capable of causing death or inflicting harm, but it does not include small pocketknives with blades of less than 2½ inches (20 U.S.C. § 930(g)(2)). The IDEA basically defines an illegal drug as a controlled substance, but the definition does not include any substance that is legally prescribed or used under the supervision of a licensed health professional (20 U.S.C. § 1415(k)(7)(A)). A controlled substance is a drug or other substance identified as such by federal law (21 U.S.C. § 812(c)). The definition of serious bodily injuries includes putting individuals at substantial risk of death, inflicting extreme physical pain, causing protracted and obvious physical disfigurement, and causing the protracted loss or impairment of the functions of bodily members, organs, or mental faculties (18 U.S.C. § 1365(h)(3)).

If parents disagree with decisions to place students in interim alternative placements, or with the particular placements themselves, and request hearings, the students are to remain in their interim alternative educational settings pending the outcome of hearings or until the expiration of the 45-day period, whichever occurs first (20 U.S.C. § 1415(k)(4)(A); 34 C.F.R. § 300.533). In any event, after the expiration of the 45-day period, the students are entitled to return to their former placements unless the parties reach other agreements or school board officials obtain injunctions barring students from their former placements. This is a modification of the IDEA's usual requirements for changing student placements. In most other situations, unless education officials and parents agree otherwise, students would remain in the educational placements they were in at the time hearings began. Students remain in these placements until all due process hearings have been completed (20 U.S.C. § 1415(j)). As discussed in the previous section, hearings that are convened over disputes regarding alternative placements must be expedited.

> If parents disagree with decisions to place students in interim alternative placements, or with the particular placements themselves, and request hearings, the students are to remain in their interim alternative educational settings pending the outcome of hearings or until the expiration of the 45-day period, whichever occurs first.

INJUNCTIONS TO REMOVE DANGEROUS OR DISRUPTIVE STUDENTS

In *Honig*, the Supreme Court granted school boards the authority to seek injunctions to exclude dangerous students with disabilities from general educational settings. The most recent IDEA amendments grant school officials another option in addition to seeking court orders. Hearing officers now have the authority to order changes in placement to appropriate interim alternative educational settings for periods of up to 45 school days when school officials can demonstrate that keeping students in their current placements is substantially likely to result in injuries to them or others (20 U.S.C. § 1415(k)(3)(B)(ii)(II); 34 C.F.R. § 300.532(b)). When making these decisions, among other factors, judges or hearing officers must consider whether school officials made reasonable efforts to minimize the risk of harm in the students' current placements.

In order to obtain *Honig* injunctions or orders from hearing officers to exclude students with disabilities, school officials must demonstrate that the students are in fact dangerous; mere allegations of dangerousness are insufficient. While it is unnecessary to demonstrate that students have inflicted injuries in the past to establish that they are potentially dangerous, school officials must present substantial credible evidence that students have the potential to inflict injuries. This may be achieved by showing that the students have committed extreme acts of misconduct that are likely to be repeated or that they committed serial acts of misconduct that escalated in their degree of seriousness. School officials must present evidence of this type in court or to hearing officers in the form of detailed disciplinary records and testimony of those who witnessed students' acts of disruption and aggression (*Clinton County R-III School District v. C. J. K.,* 1995; *Eric J. v. Huntsville City Board of Education,* 1995).

> In order to obtain *Honig* injunctions or orders from hearing officers to exclude students with disabilities, school officials must demonstrate that the students are in fact dangerous; mere allegations of dangerousness are insufficient.

According to a federal trial court in Florida (*School Board of Hillsborough County v. Student 26493257X,* 1995), school boards are not required to provide parents with any notice prior to seeking injunctions. The school board in this case had obtained a temporary restraining order to prevent the student from attending school. When the parents complained that they were not given any notice that the school board intended to pursue judicial intervention as opposed to administrative due process hearings, the court explained that requiring officials to provide presuit notice would have been contrary to the Supreme Court's holding in *Honig.* In *Honig* the Court reasoned that school boards can overcome the exhaustion requirement by showing that doing so would have been futile or inadequate. Generally speaking, the IDEA requires all parties to exhaust administrative remedies before seeking judicial relief, unless it is futile to do so. *Honig* created an exception to this requirement.

> In order to obtain injunctions to prevent students from attending their current educational programs, school personnel must show that they have done all they can to mitigate the danger or chances of disruption and that there are no less-restrictive alternatives.

In order to obtain injunctions to prevent students from attending their current educational programs, school personnel must show that they have done all they can to mitigate the danger or chances of disruption and that there are no less-restrictive alternatives (*School District of Philadelphia v. Stephan M. and Theresa M.*, 1997). Injunctions have been issued when school officials have demonstrated that students committed acts that injured themselves, other students, or staff or had the potential to cause injuries. Except in extreme circumstances, seeking injunctions cannot be the first response to acts of student misconduct. When students with disabilities misbehave, school disciplinarians should take progressive action to curb their misconduct. School officials are more likely to obtain injunctions when they can show that even though they responded appropriately to each act of misconduct, the misconduct escalated. In this respect, documentation is essential. Chapter 7 includes examples of forms that can be used for documentation in these situations.

One question that has arisen is whether the IDEA requires school officials to seek relief from hearing officers before seeking injunctions. At least one court ruled that the IDEA allows school boards to seek orders from hearing officers but does not require them to do so prior to seeking injunctions (*Gadsden City Board of Education v. B. P.*, 1998). In this dispute, the federal trial court in Alabama was of the opinion that the expedited hearing provision is permissive, and exhaustion of administrative remedies is not required if school officials choose to seek a *Honig* injunction in court.

As an alternative to seeking injunctions to remove dangerous students from schools, administrators could seek court-ordered transfers to other settings. Courts may issue *Honig*-type injunctions to allow school officials to transfer students to more restrictive programs over their parents' objections while administrative hearings are pending (*School Board of Pinellas County v. J. M. by L. M.*, 1997). The IDEA also grants hearing officers the authority to order interim alternative placements for not more than 45 school days if school personnel can demonstrate by substantial evidence that keeping students in their current placements is substantially likely to result in injuries to them or others (20 U.S.C. § 1415(k)(3)(B)(ii)(II); 34 C.F.R. § 300.532 (b)(2)(ii)). In considering these transfer requests, hearing officers are likely to consider the appropriateness of the students' current placements as well as the efforts school officials have made to minimize the risk of harm in those settings. As with interim alternative placements due to weapons or drug possession or the infliction of serious bodily injuries, interim alternative placements ordered under this provision must allow the students to continue to participate in the general education curriculum, meet their IEP goals, and receive services and modifications to address their misbehavior.

Regardless of whether they are seeking decisions from courts or hearing officers to order changes in students' placements for disciplinary reasons, school officials bear the burden of proving that such action is necessary. In order to do this, school officials must show that the students' continued presence in their current placements constitutes a danger to them or others, that educators have done all they can to curb the misbehavior in the current placements, and that programs in less restrictive environments will not meet the students' needs. For example, a federal trial court in New York issued a preliminary injunction to permit school authorities to place a student in a full-time special education classroom on a temporary basis pending completion of due process proceedings after school officials were able to show that the student was dangerous (*Binghamton City School District v. Borgna*, 1991). The student frequently exhibited aggressive behavior such as punching other children, sticking a pencil in the ear of another, throwing shoes at staff members, hitting staff members, tipping over desks, and throwing chairs. In another case where a student exhibited many behavior problems in a middle school setting, a federal trial court in Florida granted a school board's request for an injunction allowing it to transfer the student to a special education center over his parents' objections (*School Board of Pinellas County v. J. M. by L. M.*, 1997). The court was convinced that the record, which included 43 acts of aggressive behavior, supported the board's contention that the student was substantially likely to injure others if he remained in his current setting.

Another federal trial court allowed educators in Illinois to exclude a dangerous student but ordered the school board to provide 10 hours per week of home instruction that would afford the student the same opportunity to earn credits as he had in his prior placement (*Board of Education of Township High School District No. 211 v. Kurtz-Imig*, 1989). In this case, school administrators presented evidence that the student violently struck peers and threatened to kill students, teachers, and staff. A state court in New York also ordered homebound instruction when school officials were able to show that returning a student to his previous placement was substantially likely to result in injuries to himself or others (*Roslyn Union Free School District v. Geffrey W.*, 2002). The court noted that the evidence revealed that the student had run out of his classroom and school, chased other students, hit teachers and students, and chewed on sharp objects while leaning back in a chair.

In a case from Texas, school personnel sought to transfer a special education student to an alternative education program for the remainder of the school year after the student, in consort with a peer, ripped the pants off a female classmate (*Randy M. v. Texas City ISD*, 2000). The IEP team previously determined that this act of misconduct was not a manifestation of the student's disabilities, but his parents sought an injunction to prevent the transfer. The court denied the parents' request for the injunction in pointing out that the school officials' disciplinary response was entirely appropriate. The court concluded that school officials were justified in taking stern and aggressive remedial action when faced with such student conduct.

Some frequently asked questions about transferring students to more restrictive settings are summarized in Figure 5.1.

Figure 5.1   Frequently Asked Questions

Q. What can school administrators do when they feel that students with disabilities should not return to their former placements after a suspension?

A. The first thing school administrators should do is to convene students' IEP teams to explore more appropriate permanent placements. Difficulty following school rules can be an indication that students are placed improperly, particularly if the incidents leading up to the suspensions were part of patterns of misconduct. In fact, the U.S. Supreme Court in *Honig* anticipated that school officials would use the 10-day suspension as a time for IEP teams to meet with parents to review, and if necessary, revise the students' IEPs and placements. The IDEA's normal change in placement procedures should be followed.

Q. What if the parents do not agree with the recommendations of the IEP teams?

A. School officials have a variety of options. First, officials can allow students to return to their former placements. However, if school personnel think that this would be problematic, they have the option of taking their cases to either hearing officers or the courts. Regardless of the path they follow, school authorities may request orders or injunctions to bar students from attending their former programs. Hearing officers and courts could order the students to be placed in alternative settings until disputes over permanent placements are resolved.

Q: What steps should school officials take to obtain injunctions or orders from hearing officers in order to prevent dangerous students from attending school?

A. When seeking orders to change student placements, the burden is on school officials to show that keeping students in their then-current placements is likely to result in injuries to them, other students, or staff. Further, school officials must demonstrate that they have taken reasonable steps to control the behavior of students and that less restrictive alternatives are not feasible. For this purpose, thorough documentation of the history of student misconduct and the response of school officials is a must. Although hearing officers and courts recognize the need for school administrators to maintain safe school environments, they are cognizant of the IDEA's preference for placing students in the least restrictive environment.

Q. What are the special provisions for students who commit weapon, drug, or serious bodily injury violations?

A. The first action that most school administrators take under these circumstances is to issue 10-day suspensions. Nevertheless, school administrators have the authority to place students in interim alternative educational settings for up to 45 school days. The IEP teams are charged with the responsibility for determining those settings.

(Continued)

(Continued)

> **Q. Again, what if the parents disagree with the placements of the students in alternative settings? Doesn't the IDEA require that the students remain in their then-current educational placements?**
>
> **A.** No. Under these special circumstances, the students would be required to attend the recommended alternative programs until hearing officers can review the parents' complaints. In these situations, hearing officers must conduct their reviews and render their decisions under an expedited timetable.

SUMMARY

Suspensions and expulsions are not the only options available to school officials who are concerned with keeping dangerous or disruptive students with disabilities in general school settings. The first option in any situation where students are continuously presenting behavioral problems is for school officials to convene students' IEP teams to evaluate whether the students' current placements are meeting their needs and providing an appropriate education. If necessary, educators can revise students' current IEPs and placements by following the IDEA's normal due process procedures.

Under special circumstances students with disabilities may be transferred to interim alternative educational settings for periods of up to 45 school days even over the objections of their parents. Those special circumstances occur when students are in possession of weapons or drugs at school or during school functions or when students commit acts that inflict serious bodily injuries. Even when parents object to these alternative placements, students must remain in these alternative settings until the end of the 45-day period or hearing officers issue orders to the contrary.

In circumstances where students are truly dangerous and must be removed from their educational settings immediately, school authorities may obtain orders from hearing officers or courts that prevent the students from continuing in their current placements. Hearing officers or courts would most likely order such students to attend some type of alternative programs.

RECOMMENDATIONS FOR PRACTITIONERS

- Maintain detailed disciplinary records on all students.
- Prior to making any changes in placement, be sure to provide parents with all required procedural safeguards, such as notice, consistent with federal and state law.

- Determine whether reevaluations are warranted prior to making any proposals to change students' placements.
- Review FBAs and BIPs to make sure that they are current and appropriate.
- Consider placing students in interim alternative educational settings for periods of up to 45 school days for violations involving weapons, drugs, or the infliction of serious bodily injury.
- Prior to seeking a court or hearing officer order to remove a dangerous student, be sure that all steps have been taken to minimize the risk of harm in the student's current placement.
- Check state laws and regulations to see if they impose any additional requirements regarding the transfer of students with disabilities to alternative placements for disciplinary reasons.

WHAT'S NEXT

The next chapter examines other, less restrictive means of discipline. The chapter will also present information regarding some of the IDEA's other disciplinary provisions, such as how to treat students who claim to have disabilities but whose disabilities have not been identified as such. Further, the chapter discusses the relationship between the schools and the courts regarding students with disabilities.

REFERENCES

Andress v. Cleveland Independent School District, 64 F.3d 176 (5th Cir. 1995).

Binghamton City School District v. Borgna, 17 EHLR 677 (N.D. N.Y. 1991).

Board of Education of Township High School District No. 211 v. Kurtz-Imig, 16 EHLR 17 (N.D. Ill. 1989).

Boggus Letter, 20 IDELR 625 (OSEP 1993).

Clinton County R-III School District v. C. J. K., 896 F. Supp. 948 (W.D. Mo. 1995).

Code of Federal Regulations (C.F.R.), as cited.

Eric J. v. Huntsville City Board of Education, 22 IDELR 858 (N.D. Ala. 1995).

Gadsden City Board of Education v. B. P., 3 F. Supp.2d 1299 (N.D. Ala. 1998).

Gun-Free School Zones Act of 1990, 20 U.S.C. § 921 *et seq.* (2006).

Honig v. Doe, 484 U.S. 305 (1988).

Individuals with Disabilities Education Act (IDEA), 20 U.S.C. §§ 1400–1482 (2006).

Jonathan G. v. Caddo Parish School Board, 875 F. Supp. 352 (W.D. La. 1994).

OCR memorandum: Long-term suspension or expulsion of handicapped students, EHLR 307:05 (1989).

Osborne, A. G., & Russo, C. J. (2007). *Special education and the law: A guide for practitioners* (2nd ed.). Thousand Oaks, CA: Corwin.

Randy M. v. Texas City ISD, 93 F. Supp.2d 1310, (S.D. Tex. 2000).

Rehabilitation Act, Section 504, 29 U.S.C. § 794 (2006).

Roslyn Union Free School District v. Geffrey W., 740 N.Y.S.2d 451 (N.Y. App. Div. 2002).

School Board of Hillsborough County v. Student 26493257X, 23 IDELR 93 (M.D. Fla. 1995).

School Board of Pinellas County v. J. M. by L. M., 957 F. Supp. 1252 (M.D. Fla. 1997).

School Board of the County of Prince William v. Wills, 16 EHLR 1109 (Va. Cir. Ct. 1989).

School Board of the County of Stafford v. Farley, 16 EHLR 1119 (Va. Cir. Ct. 1990).

School District of Philadelphia v. Stephan M. and Theresa M., 1997 WL 89113 (E.D. Pa. 1997).

United States Code (U.S.C.), as cited.

6 Other Disciplinary Considerations

INTRODUCTION

Suspensions, expulsions, and transfers to interim alternative educational settings are arguably the most drastic disciplinary sanctions school officials can impose on students with disabilities. Yet, they are not the only disciplinary tools available. Educators frequently employ tactics such as detentions, the use of time-out rooms, and in-school suspensions as a means of responding to minor infractions of school rules. In states that allow it, school disciplinarians may even employ corporal punishment. Further, in an effort to curb misbehavior before it escalates, school personnel may adjust students' schedules. As noted in Chapter 2, even these seemingly minor disciplinary tactics have been subject to litigation.

An issue that has been the focus of a great deal of controversy is whether students who have not been identified as having disabilities, but who claim to be disabled, have the same rights under the Individuals with Disabilities Education Act (IDEA, 2006) as peers who are already receiving special education services. The controversy stems from the fact that parents often raise the issue of students having previously unidentified disabilities only after school officials seek to impose disciplinary sanctions. The IDEA now specifically addresses this issue. A related question that is not directly addressed in the IDEA concerns whether former special education students who are no longer covered by individualized education programs (IEPs) retain their rights when facing discipline. The answers often depend on the circumstances.

In many cases, infractions of school rules are also violations of states' criminal codes. For example, when individuals possess weapons or drugs or subject others to serious physical assaults, they typically can be charged with criminal offenses. When these violations occur, school officials usually work in tandem with the local police and juvenile authorities to investigate the incidents and take appropriate action. Depending on the circumstances, criminal charges may be brought in addition to whatever action is taken by school personnel. The IDEA also addresses this situation.

This chapter analyzes miscellaneous disciplinary provisions in the IDEA along with other issues that may arise in the school setting. The chapter begins with a review of litigation on minor disciplinary sanctions that officials commonly impose on students with disabilities. The chapter next covers the related topics of the rights of both students who have yet to be identified as having disabilities and those who are no longer receiving services under IEPs. The chapter concludes with an examination of the interaction between school systems and the juvenile justice system.

MINOR DISCIPLINARY SANCTIONS

School officials may impose typical minor disciplinary sanctions, such as detentions or the use of time-out areas, on students with disabilities without resorting to the IDEA's procedures as long as the sanctions are the same as those applied to children who are not disabled under similar circumstances. In fact, the IDEA makes it clear that officials can mete out more serious sanctions to students with disabilities as long as the sanctions are the same as for those who do not have disabilities (20 U.S.C. § 1415(k)(1)(B); 34 C.F.R. § 300.530(b)). It is certainly reasonable to assume that the same principle would apply for minor disciplinary actions. However, school officials are advised that while it is not required, it is prudent to identify the disciplinary sanctions that are to be used in the behavior intervention plans (BIPs) or IEPs of students with a propensity for disruptiveness. Educators who outline the disciplinary tactics in students' BIPs in advance and have them agreed to by the parents can avoid many questions later should problems arise.

Detentions

Detentions, or keeping students after school, are commonly used as disciplinary tools in schools. Many school administrators have found detentions to be effective in curbing minor disciplinary infractions. As normal disciplinary procedures that are used with all students, detentions do not seem to pose a problem when used with special education students (*Walpole Public Schools*, 1995). To this end, a Department of Education policy letter explained that after-school detentions do not

> As normal disciplinary procedures that are used with all students, detentions do not seem to pose a problem when used with special education students.

constitute significant changes in placements (*Williams Letter*, 1994). Still, the letter stresses that any significant patterns of disciplinary actions for behavior caused by disabilities could be sufficient cause to believe that educators have violated Section 504 of the Rehabilitation Act (Rehabilitation Act, Section 504, 2006). The bottom line is that officials should not continue to issue serial detentions without taking other steps to address the students' misbehavior.

The fact that educators can use detentions as occasional tools in disciplining students with disabilities aside, there is an important related safety consideration to keep in mind. More specifically, insofar as many students with disabilities receive transportation as a related service under their IEPs, officials should take steps to ensure that students do not miss their rides home. In fact, although no cases could be found on this point, inasmuch as transportation is a required related service, when detentions are assigned, school boards may still be required to transport the students home, particularly if transportation is included in the students' IEPs. Moreover, to the extent that parents may expect their children home at a set time each day, educators would be wise not to impose detention on the day that a student commits an infraction. Rather, school officials should notify parents that their children will be punished over the next week or so in order that they can arrange alternative transportation, if necessary, to ensure that their children arrive home safely.

Time-Outs and In-School Suspensions

Special educators who teach students with behavior problems commonly employ a technique known as "time-out" as part of a behavior modification program. Time-outs refer to the removal of students from their usual settings for specified and limited periods of time. The students are usually placed in secluded areas of the classrooms set aside for this purpose or in separate time-out rooms. Time-outs are considered to be minor disciplinary sanctions unless the length of the time-outs is excessive (Seiden & Zirkel, 1989). Similarly, in-school suspensions are also commonly used when students commit minor infractions, particularly if the misconduct was a first offense. While students are required to attend school and complete classroom assignments during in-school suspensions, instead of attending their normal classes, they generally are required to remain in the schools' offices or other designated areas isolated from other students.

For the most part, time-outs or in-school suspensions do not trigger the IDEA's due process safeguards as long as they are temporary and for specified, minimal amounts of time (Lincoln, 1989). In such a case, the Tenth Circuit held that such short-term disciplinary measures as time-outs or in-school suspensions generally do not constitute changes in placements (*Hayes v. Unified School District No. 377*, 1989). Even so, the court indicated that in-class disciplinary methods, since they are matters relating to the education of the child, are subject to the IDEA's administrative appeals process if the parents raise objections. Again, although not required, it is recommended that if such methods are to be used, they should be outlined in students' BIPs and/or IEPs. As with the issue of detention, school officials should be careful to ensure that students in time-out or in-school suspension situations are properly supervised (Mawdsley, 2001). In one case parents from Colorado filed suit against school personnel who had placed a student in a closet unsupervised for time-out in contradiction to the terms of her IEP. While in the closet the student fell and severely injured her head. The Tenth Circuit, although not condoning the actions of the school's staff, ruled that damages were not available under the IDEA (*Padilla v. School District No. 1 in the City and County of Denver*, 2000). Even so, monetary damages could be available in such a situation under state tort laws.

A federal trial court in Tennessee ruled that a time-out did not violate a student's right to an education (*Dickens v. Johnson County Board of Education*, 1987). Similarly, the Eighth Circuit, in a dispute from Arkansas, insisted that an in-school suspension, even when it limited a student's access to special

> For the most part, time-outs or in-school suspensions do not trigger the IDEA's due process safeguards as long as they are temporary and for specified, minimal amounts of time.

education classes and resources, did not violate his rights to substantive due process (*Wise v. Pea Ridge School District*, 1988). The court emphasized that an in-school suspension furthered the school board's legitimate interest in maintaining order and discipline. On the other hand, the Department of Education wrote in a policy letter that in-school disciplinary measures that remove students from their educational programs are to be treated as suspensions (*Williams Letter*, 1994). Presumably, such in-school suspensions would be subject to the IDEA's 10-day limit. By the same token, as noted by a federal trial court in Alabama, educators may assume that in-school suspensions are not counted toward the 10-day limit when the students receive special education services during the in-school suspension periods (*Eric J. v. Huntsville City Board of Education*, 1995). School officials must be cautioned that excessive use of in-school suspensions, even those during which students are provided with special education services, may be viewed as creating patterns of exclusion from the students' usual learning environments. When such patterns develop for behaviors that are manifestations of students' disabilities, they can also be treated as violations of Section 504 (*Williams Letter*, 1994).

The IDEA does not limit school administrators' rights to use normal disciplinary sanctions, short of expulsion, with special education students. Still, educators should check to see whether their state policies may impose other restrictions. For example, some states may limit the number of days students may be placed on in-school suspensions if they are not allowed to attend special education classes while suspended. If students are being deprived of special education services, even for short periods of time, states may treat in-school suspensions in the same manner as out-of-building suspensions, so that they would count toward the 10-day limitation placed on suspensions. Although the IDEA's 10-day limit on suspensions is consecutive, rather than cumulative, individual states may impose other restrictions on the total number of days special education students may be suspended in one school year. Under equal protection analysis, states may reduce this number but may not increase it, since doing so would limit the protections that the IDEA affords. Educators in such states need to be aware that in-school suspensions without access to students' special education programs may count as suspension days in this regard.

A judgment of an appellate court in Pennsylvania illustrates the fact that it is a disciplinary measure's effect that determines whether it violates the IDEA. The court affirmed that an in-school suspension amounted to a *de facto* or constructive suspension when the student chose to go home rather than report for the in-school suspension (*Big Beaver Falls Area School District v. Jackson*, 1993). The court was convinced that since educators continued to assign in-school suspensions after it became abundantly clear that the student would opt to go home, they knew that an in-school suspension would have resulted in her exclusion. Insofar as the total number of days the student was excluded from school exceeded the maximum allowed by commonwealth law, the court pointed out that school officials acted contrary to the IDEA's mandates regarding student exclusions.

Modified or Reduced Day Schedules

It is not an uncommon practice for school officials to place continually disruptive students on modified or reduced day schedules based on the notion that their misbehavior may be caused by an inability to tolerate a full day of instruction. Officials may act in this manner only after they have complied with the IDEA's change in placement procedures, since doing otherwise would constitute a substantial modification to the students' programs (*Doe v. Maher*, 1986). Thus, before IEP teams may place students with disabilities on reduced day schedules, they must follow the IDEA's due process procedures. These procedures include written notice to parents of intended actions (20 U.S.C. § 1415(b)(3)). If parents disagree with contemplated actions, they may request due process hearings (20 U.S.C. § 1415(f)). When parents request hearings, educators may not change student placements absent parental consent or orders from courts or hearing officers (20 U.S.C. § 1415(j)). Further, Section 504 requires a reevaluation before any significant changes in placement occur (34 C.F.R. § 104.35(a)).

> It is not an uncommon practice for school officials to place continually disruptive students on modified or reduced day schedules based on the notion that their misbehavior may be caused by an inability to tolerate a full day of instruction.

Precedent exists for placing students with disabilities on a modified schedule in nondisciplinary situations. For instance, the Fifth Circuit affirmed that a school board in Texas was not required to provide a student who had multiple disabilities with a full day of instruction where a full day was not in his best interests (*Christopher M. v. Corpus Christi Independent School District*, 1991). The court acknowledged that there is no requirement that students with disabilities be provided with full days of instruction. The record reflected the fact the school personnel determined that the student was unable to tolerate a full day of educational programming. The same principle would apply to students who have behavioral difficulties. When dealing with similar situations, school administrators must be cautioned that any changes to give students modified schedules should be proposed for programmatic or therapeutic reasons and not as punishment.

Corporal Punishment

As discussed in Chapter 2, common law allows school officials to impose reasonable corporal punishment unless it is prohibited by state law (Russo, 2006). At present, corporal punishment is permitted in twenty-two states (Randall, 2008). Again, as a normal disciplinary tool, corporal punishment may be used with special education students as long as it is applied in the same manner as it would be for students who do not have disabilities. When courts evaluate the reasonableness of corporal punishment, they typically consider the nature of students' offenses, the punishments inflicted, and students' ages and sizes (Underwood & Mead, 1995). Educators may be sued, typically for civil liability, if they use excessive corporal punishment, especially if they violate state law or board policy (Russo, 2006).

> Common law allows school officials to impose reasonable corporal punishment unless it is prohibited by state law. . . . As a normal disciplinary tool, corporal punishment may be used with special education students as long as it is applied in the same manner as it would be for students who do not have disabilities.

A federal trial court in Indiana, a state that authorizes corporal punishment, maintained that paddling a student with disabilities, taping his mouth, and providing him with an isolated seating arrangement did not violate his rights (*Cole v. Greenfield-Central Community Schools*, 1986). In finding that these punishments were not excessive and were within school officials' common law privileges, the court thought that the educators were entitled to substantial discretion in handling day-to-day discipline. The court noted that the student received the same punishment any other child would have received. The judge went so far as to remark that "an elementary school cannot be subjugated by the tyrannical behavior of a nine-year-old child" (p. 63).

An unfortunate situation in Michigan provides an example of the care school officials need to exercise whenever physical punishment is contemplated. The teacher of a student with a congenital heart defect and orthopedic disabilities forced him to run a 350-yard sprint as punishment for talking in line (*Waechter v. School District No. 14–030 of Cassopolis*, 1991). The student suffered cardiac arrhythmia while making the run and died. School personnel were well aware of the student's physical condition and the restrictions his physician imposed regarding physical exertion. The student's parents sued for damages, alleging violations of their son's Fourteenth Amendment due process rights, Section 504, and the state's wrongful death statute. Although the court ruled that damages were not available under Section 504, it allowed the parents' allegations of substantive, but not procedural, due process violations to continue. The court added that school officials were not protected by qualified immunity.

Physical Restraints

Although not a disciplinary sanction, school administrators and special educators frequently must apply physical restraints to students who are unruly. The IDEA does not address the use of physical restraints, but this topic is generally governed by state law or regulations. By way of illustration, Massachusetts regulations provide very strict guidelines on the use of physical restraint in the public schools (Code of Massachusetts Regulations, 2008). Those regulations require school officials to notify parents and file written reports with the commonwealth's Department of Education on every physical restraint that lasts longer than 20 minutes or that causes an injury to a student or staff member that requires medical intervention. Further, the Massachusetts regulations require training for all staff members in the school system's physical restraint policies and in-depth training in the use of physical restraint for designated staff members in each school building. Only school personnel who have been given this in-depth training may administer physical restraints in Massachusetts.

Educators should include the use of physical restraints in students' IEPs or BIPs if its use is contemplated. Although not a guarantee, including physical restraint in IEPs or BIPs provides a level of protection from suits for damages in the event that parents sue school personnel who have used physical restraints on their children. Being properly trained in the use of physical restraints also provides a degree of protection from liability should students be injured while restrained. Trained personnel are more likely to use only the minimum amount of restraint necessary to control the students and thus have a decreased chance of inflicting injury in the process. For example, a federal trial court in Virginia dismissed a suit filed against a teacher and a classroom aide by the parents of a student who had been restrained (*Brown v. Ramsey*, 2000). The student's IEP stated that physical restraint would be used if he became a danger to himself or others. Further, the court did not find any evidence that the student had been injured during restraints. In another situation the Eighth Circuit concluded that the use of a blanket wrapping technique recommended by a physical therapist to calm a student did not violate a student's right to be free from unreasonable bodily restraint (*Heidemann v. Rother*, 1996). On the other hand, a federal trial court in New York allowed a suit to go forward after finding evidence that the force a teacher used was disproportionate to the need presented (*Dockery v. Barnett*, 2001).

Physical restraints may be used when necessary to protect students and staff from danger. In the Virginia case discussed in the previous paragraph, the student's IEP specifically provided for restraints to be used if the student became a danger to himself or others. In a case from Texas, a federal trial court dismissed an action filed against school officials who had wrapped an out-of-control student in a blanket for safety reasons (*Doe v. S & S Consolidated Independent School District*, 2001). The court was convinced that the student's substantive due process rights did not give her the right to be free from restraints used to control her outbursts so as to prevent harm to herself and to those charged with the responsibility for her education. In another situation, the federal trial court in Connecticut agreed that school personnel who had implemented restraints in response to a student's misbehavior exercised professional judgment. The court was thus satisfied that educators acted in accordance with professionally accepted standards (*M. H. by Mr. and Mrs. H. v. Bristol Board of Education*, 2002).

RIGHTS OF STUDENTS NOT YET IDENTIFIED AS HAVING DISABILITIES

Prior to the enactment of the 1997 IDEA amendments, courts were divided on the issue of how students should be treated who had not been identified as being eligible for special education at the time the disciplinary action arose yet alleged that they had previously unidentified disabilities. The statute and its regulations now mandate that the IDEA's protections must be afforded to such students if school officials knew that they had disabilities before their misbehavior occurred (20 U.S.C. § 1415(k)(5)(A); 34 C.F.R. § 300.534(a)). Further, the IDEA delineates the criteria under which school personnel are deemed to have had such knowledge. Factors such as parents' expressed written concern that the students may require special education or parental requests for an evaluation and teachers' or other staff's specific expressed concerns about the students' patterns of behavior are all indicators that school officials had reason to know that the students had disabilities (20 U.S.C. § 1415(k)(5)(B); 34 C.F.R. § 300.534(b)).

> Prior to the enactment of the 1997 IDEA amendments, courts were divided on the issue of how students should be treated who had not been identified as being eligible for special education at the time the disciplinary action arose yet alleged that they had previously unidentified disabilities.

Exceptions to the above exist when the parents of the students have refused to allow school boards to conduct evaluations of their children or have previously refused special education services. Moreover, school boards are not deemed to have had knowledge of disabilities if they conducted evaluations and determined that the students did not have disabilities (20 U.S.C. § 1415(k)(5)(C); 34 C.F.R. § 300.534(c)).

If school boards did not have prior knowledge that the students had disabilities, they may be disciplined in the same manner as their peers (20 U.S.C. § 1415(k)(5)(D)(i); 34 C.F.R. § 300.534(d)(1)). However, if evaluations are requested during a time period in which disciplinary sanctions have been imposed, officials must conduct these evaluations in an expedited manner (20 U.S.C. § 1415(k)(5)(D)(ii); 34 C.F.R. § 300.535(d)(2)). While evaluations are being conducted, students are to remain in the educational placements determined by school authorities, which could be suspensions or expulsions (20 U.S.C. § 1415(k)(5)(D)(ii); 34 C.F.R. § 300.534(d)(2)(ii)). The fact that students may have been suspended or expelled should not be used to delay the completion of requested evaluations. If students are found to have disabilities, school boards must provide them with special education and related services in accordance with the terms of the IDEA (34 C.F.R. § 300.534(d)(2)(iii)).

Evaluating whether school personnel had prior knowledge that students were eligible for special education can be tricky. For example, as shown by a decision from a federal trial court in Mississippi, prior requests for evaluations by themselves may not always be sufficient reasons to assume that students do have disabilities. The court upheld the expulsion of a student who had been diagnosed as having attention deficit disorder (*Colvin v. Lowndes County, Mississippi School District*, 1999). Even though his parents made a request for an evaluation, the court was not convinced that the student had disabilities. It is important to keep in mind that this case was litigated before the IDEA specifically identified the circumstances under which school officials would be deemed to have knowledge of disabilities. On the other hand, a federal trial court in Connecticut asserted that school officials had knowledge that a student had a disability because his parents expressed concern over his poor performance and requested an evaluation (*J. C. v. Regional School District No. 10*, 2000). The student was evaluated a second time and was found to be in need of special education, a fact that undoubtedly influenced the court's analysis. The point is that it is better to err on the side of caution so that if requests for evaluations are on file, school officials should deem themselves as having had knowledge that the students may have had disabilities.

According to the IDEA, if students were not previously identified as having disabilities, then school boards are not considered to have had prior knowledge that students were eligible for special education. Even so, IEP teams' determinations that students do not have disabilities may be insufficient to show that the students are not eligible for special education, especially if the actions of IEP teams are appealed or are later shown to have been incorrect. In a case where a student failed all of her courses, the federal trial court in Massachusetts observed that although there could have been a variety of reasons why a student might have failed courses, one of them could be the possibility of her having a disability (*S. W. and Joanne W. v. Holbrook Public Schools*, 2002). The court thus decided that the student's allegations were sufficient to present a viable claim that school officials had knowledge that she had disabilities even though the IEP team disagreed. It is important to recognize that this inclusion to the criteria for having knowledge that students have disabilities was added as part of the 2004 amendments, two years after the court rendered its judgment. In light of the current wording in the IDEA, it is unclear how a court would rule when IEP teams erroneously determine that students do not have disabilities. Certainly, school boards would be hard pressed to defend themselves for not providing the IDEA's protections under the guise of lacking knowledge that students had disabilities when that position was based on the erroneous judgments of IEP teams.

As the above cases indicate, students who claim to have disabilities may not have a difficult time proving their point. Most courts would rather err on the side of assuming that students have disabilities rather than potentially deprive them of statutorily defined rights. There is an old adage that it is better to provide more process than is due. That is good advice in situations of this type. If there are any questions whether students may be eligible for special education, it would be prudent for educators to treat them as if they had disabilities and provide all of the due process mandated by the IDEA.

Again, this is an area that may be affected by state law. For example, Michigan has recently enacted legislation that requires school boards to immediately evaluate any students they have reasonable cause to suspect are eligible for special education, prior to taking disciplinary action, if they are contemplating suspending or expelling those students (Michigan Revised School Code, 2007).

RIGHTS OF FORMER SPECIAL EDUCATION STUDENTS

The IDEA does not directly address the related issue of whether former special education students, who were no longer receiving special education and related services at the time disciplinary sanctions were imposed, are entitled to the protections of the IDEA. The answer may depend on the circumstances surrounding the students' withdrawals from special education programs.

An early opinion written by a federal trial court in Wisconsin indicates that students who are no longer receiving special education services may still be covered by the IDEA in the eyes of the law. The student at issue was removed from a special education class for students with emotional problems at the request of

> The IDEA does not directly address the related issue of whether former special education students, who were no longer receiving special education and related services at the time disciplinary sanctions were imposed, are entitled to the protections of the IDEA.

his parent but against the recommendation of school personnel (*Steldt v. School Board of the Riverdale School District*, 1995). School administrators subsequently expelled the student for a series of acts that included assaults on fellow students, a teacher, and the principal. The court declared that the student was entitled to the protections of the IDEA, because he was still a student in need of special education in spite of his parent's request that he be removed from special education. In the court's view, the student was still a student with disabilities entitled to the protections of the IDEA.

Insofar as there is an unfortunate dearth of litigation on this subject, school officials are left with almost no guidance. It is important to note that *Steldt* above was decided before the IDEA's disciplinary provisions were incorporated into the statute. In light of other provisions in the IDEA, it is difficult to predict how courts would rule on cases involving former special education students today. Judicial orders will hinge largely on the unique circumstances of each case and how well school officials documented their positions.

As indicated in the previous paragraph, it is difficult to predict how courts are likely to respond to situations where students are unilaterally removed from special education by their parents against the advice of IEP teams. On the one hand, as shown earlier in this chapter, the IDEA specifically indicates that school boards are not deemed to have known that students had disabilities when parents refused their consent for requested evaluations or rejected proposed special education services (20 U.S.C. § 1415(k)(5)(C); 34 C.F.R. § 300.534(c)). It is highly conceivable that courts could extend that provision to reason that students whose parents have unilaterally removed them from special education are no longer protected by the IDEA. Conversely, it is not out of the realm of possibility that courts would still consider such students as having disabilities in spite of their parents' actions. Sympathetic courts could be inclined to give students the benefit of the doubt in situations such as this, particularly where their rights may have been compromised by actions of their parents over which the students themselves had no control. Further, even though these students may no longer be receiving services under the IDEA, as students with disabilities they would still be entitled to protections against discrimination under Section 504.

It is also impossible to predict how courts would respond to students who were deemed to be no longer eligible for special education by their IEP teams but claimed to still have disabilities when school officials imposed disciplinary actions. Students in such situations would likely be required to remain in their disciplinary placements, such as suspensions or expulsions, while they challenged the determinations of their IEP teams that they were no longer eligible for special education. Again in a situation of this type, school boards would be in a difficult position if they had to try to defend actions that were taken based on decisions by IEP teams that erroneously concluded that students were no longer eligible for special education.

EFFECT ON THE JUVENILE COURT AND LAW ENFORCEMENT AGENCIES

The current version of the IDEA states that nothing in the statute can be interpreted as prohibiting school officials from reporting crimes committed by special education students to the proper authorities or to impede law enforcement and judicial authorities from carrying out their responsibilities (20 U.S.C. § 1415(k)(6)(A); 34 C.F.R. § 300.535(a)). If school officials do report crimes, the IDEA also requires them to furnish the students' special education and disciplinary records to the appropriate authorities (20 U.S.C. § 1415(k)(6)(B); 34 C.F.R. § 300.535(b)). In such a situation, an appellate court in Massachusetts affirmed that the IDEA clearly authorized school officials to report criminal activities to the appropriate authorities (*Commonwealth v. Nathaniel N.*, 2002).

> The current version of the IDEA states that nothing in the statute can be interpreted as prohibiting school officials from reporting crimes committed by special education students to the proper authorities or to impede law enforcement and judicial authorities from carrying out their responsibilities.

On more than one occasion students with disabilities unsuccessfully claimed that their being adjudicated delinquent, and subsequent incarcerations in the juvenile system, constituted changes in placements under the IDEA. A student from Massachusetts failed in such an attempt after he was prosecuted for possession of marijuana (*Commonwealth v. Nathaniel N.*, 2002). Previously, a student from Wisconsin unsuccessfully charged that school officials were required to utilize the IDEA's administrative hearing process before they could file a juvenile delinquency petition for alleged behavior that occurred in school (*In re Trent N.*, 1997). An appellate court emphasized that the IDEA is targeted toward school action, not toward the state's statutory authority to file a delinquency petition.

On the other hand, school officials cannot use the juvenile justice system as a means of avoiding their responsibilities to students under the IDEA, particularly in situations where the students have not violated states' criminal codes. A family court in New York declared that a person in need of services (PINS) proceeding that school officials initiated due to a student's tardiness, absenteeism, and misbehavior constituted a change in placement under the IDEA (*In re Doe*, 2002). The court was of the opinion that officials should have initiated an IEP meeting to evaluate whether additional interventions or modifications to the student's IEP were warranted before seeking to remove him from his then-current educational placement by filing the PINS petition. In an early case, an appellate court in Tennessee reversed actions taken by school officials that resulted in a student's being adjudicated as unruly and placed in the custody of the state's Department of Human Services (*In re Tony McCann*, 1990). The court was convinced that school administrators should have taken steps to find an appropriate educational placement for the student before resorting to the courts.

Some frequently asked questions about disciplinary considerations are summarized in Figure 6.1.

Figure 6.1   Frequently Asked Questions

Q. Are there any restrictions on using detentions and time-outs on students with disabilities?

A. As long as educators use disciplinary sanctions on students with disabilities to the same degree and extent as they do so on students who do not have disabilities under similar circumstances, there should not be a problem. Still, educators should review the IEPs and placements of students with disabilities who constitute ongoing behavior problems. Continuing to hand out punishments without taking steps to address the underlying behavior could be problematic under some circumstances in that it might indicate that officials failed to offer an appropriate education.

Q. Do in-school suspensions count toward the 10-day limit on suspensions?

A. As long as the students are not denied access to their special education programs and are given the opportunity to complete assignments and progress in the general education curriculum during in-school suspensions, they would most likely not be counted toward the 10-day limit. However, serial suspensions of any sort, without other intervening actions, may be considered changes in placement under the IDEA. In this respect, serial removals from the students' educational environments, even via in-school suspensions, can be problematic. Further, state laws may impose additional restrictions on the use of in-school suspensions.

Q. Can students who have never been identified as having disabilities avoid disciplinary action by claiming to have previously undiagnosed disabilities?

A. Students who have never shown an indication that they have disabilities generally cannot invoke the IDEA as a means of avoiding disciplinary consequences. Yet, if teachers or parents expressed concerns in writing about the students in the past so that school officials had reason to suspect the students had disabilities, the students would be entitled to the IDEA's protections. The IDEA's disciplinary protections are designed to ensure that students with disabilities are not denied their right to free appropriate public educations as a consequence of disciplinary actions. The IDEA was not designed to allow students who do not have disabilities to avoid disciplinary sanctions.

Q. May school administrators report crimes committed by students with disabilities on school grounds to the proper juvenile authorities?

A. Absolutely. In fact, the IDEA requires school officials to report crimes regardless of whether the students who committed them have disabilities and are protected by the IDEA. Conversely, educators cannot use the juvenile system to avoid their responsibilities under the IDEA, particularly when students have not committed crimes. Courts are not inclined to approve so-called unruly petitions when school personnel have failed to do all that they could to meet students' needs within the school system.

SUMMARY

School officials can confidently use minor disciplinary procedures, such as time-outs, detentions, and corporal punishments in states that allow it, on students with disabilities without any need to provide additional due process protections as long as these sanctions are used to the same extent as they would be used under similar circumstances for students who do not have disabilities. When punishments become excessive, educators should be concerned, because, at this point, they should consider reviewing the students' IEPs and programs to evaluate whether they are meeting the students' needs. Similarly, in-school suspensions do not require any extra procedural steps, particularly if students are still able to access their special education services during suspension periods.

Students who have not been identified as having disabilities lack an entitlement to the protections of the IDEA, unless school officials had knowledge that they might have disabilities. If such knowledge exists, educators would be prudent to treat students as if they have already been identified as having disabilities and provide them with all of the IDEA's safeguards.

Nothing in the IDEA prevents school officials from reporting misconduct that qualifies as a crime to juvenile authorities or cooperating with juvenile authorities in ensuing investigations. The fact that students may be identified as having disabilities does not provide them with additional protections in the juvenile justice system.

RECOMMENDATIONS FOR PRACTITIONERS

- When imposing minor disciplinary sanctions, such as detentions, be sure that the punishment for students with disabilities is the same as would be meted out to their peers under similar circumstances.
- In developing students' IEPs and BIPs, contemplate the types of disciplinary sanctions that will be used and include these in the written documents.
- Make sure that students in time-out areas or in-school suspension rooms are properly supervised at all times.
- Continue to provide special education services to students with disabilities who are serving in-school suspensions.
- Check state laws to see if there are any provisions regarding the use of in-school suspensions and whether these count toward the total number of days a student with disabilities may be suspended before triggering the IDEA's change in placement provisions.
- Before implementing any modified or reduced day schedules, be sure that this is the recommendation of the IEP team and that you

have parental consent. As a change in placement, a modified schedule is subject to the IDEA's due process procedures.

- Exercise extreme caution in using corporal punishment with students with disabilities inasmuch as the nature of their disabilities may lead to greater liability on the part of disciplinarians.
- Implement physical restraints only to the extent necessary to prevent injury or as directed in students' IEPs.
- Provide proper training to all staff who are in a position to implement physical restraints.
- Check state laws and regulations to see what reporting requirements, if any, exist when physical restraints are used.
- Do not continue to issue serial disciplinary sanctions of any kind without first reconvening students' IEP teams to determine if their current placements and programs are adequately meeting their needs.
- Given the old adage that it is always better to provide more process than is due, if there are any questions regarding students' status as having disabilities, implement all of the IDEA's requirements before administering discipline. In other words treat students who have not yet been identified as having disabilities and former special education students as if they were students with disabilities if there is any question whatsoever about their status.
- Fully cooperate with juvenile justice authorities and juvenile courts when a student with disabilities commits an act of misbehavior that also constitutes a crime.

WHAT'S NEXT

The next chapter summarizes the IDEA's disciplinary provisions and offers practical suggestions for implementing the procedures outlined in the IDEA and its regulations. The chapter also includes sample forms and notices that can be used during the disciplinary process.

REFERENCES

Big Beaver Falls Area School District v. Jackson, 624 A.2d 806 (Pa. Commw. Ct. 1993).
Brown v. Ramsey, 121 F. Supp.2d 911 (E.D. Va. 2000).
Christopher M. v. Corpus Christi Independent School District, 933 F.2d 1285 (5th Cir. 1991).
Code of Federal Regulations (C.F.R.), as cited.
Code of Massachusetts Regulations, Chapter 603, Section 46 (2008).
Cole v. Greenfield-Central Community Schools, 657 F. Supp. 56 (S.D. Ind. 1986).
Colvin v. Lowndes County, Mississippi School District, 114 F. Supp.2d 504 (N.D. Miss. 1999).

Commonwealth v. Nathaniel N., 764 N.E.2d 883 (Mass. Ct. App. 2002).

Dickens v. Johnson County Board of Education, 661 F. Supp. 155 (E.D. Tenn. 1987).

Dockery v. Barnett, 167 F. Supp.2d 597 (S.D. N.Y. 2001).

Doe, In re, 753 N.Y.S.2d 656 (N.Y. Fam. Ct. 2002).

Doe v. Maher, 793 F.2d 1470 (9th Cir. 1986), *affirmed sub nom. Honig v. Doe,* 484 U.S. 305 (1988).

Doe v. S & S Consolidated Independent School District, 149 F. Supp.2d 274 (E.D. Tex. 2001).

Eric J. v. Huntsville City Board of Education, 22 IDELR 858 (N.D. Ala. 1995).

Hayes v. Unified School District No. 377, 877 F.2d 809 (10th Cir. 1989).

Heidemann v. Rother, 84 F.3d 1021 (8th Cir. 1996).

Individuals with Disabilities Education Act (IDEA), 20 U.S.C. §§ 1400–1482 (2006).

J. C. v. Regional School District No. 10, 115 F. Supp.2d 297 (D. Conn. 2000), *reversed on other grounds,* 278 F.3d 119 (2d Cir. 2002).

Lincoln, E. A. (1989). Disciplining handicapped students: Questions unanswered in *Honig v. Doe. Education Law Reporter, 51,* 1–9.

Mawdsley, R. (2001). Standard of care and students with disabilities. *Education Law Reporter, 148,* 553–571.

M. H. by Mr. and Mrs. H. v. Bristol Board of Education, 2002 WL 33802431 (D. Conn. 2002).

Michigan Revised School Code, 380 M.C.L. § 1311(1) (2007).

Padilla v. School District No. 1 in the City and County of Denver, 233 F.3d 1268 (10th Cir. 2000).

Randall, D. (2008). *States with corporal punishment in school.* Retrieved July 31, 2008, from http://school.familyeducation.com/classroom-discipline/resource/38377.html

Rehabilitation Act, Section 504, 29 U.S.C. § 794 (2006).

Russo, C. J. (2006). *Reutter's the law of public education.* New York: Foundation Press.

Seiden, S. B., & Zirkel, P. A. (1989). Aversive therapy for handicapped students. *Education Law Reporter, 48,* 1029–1044.

Steldt v. School Board of the Riverdale School District, 885 F. Supp. 1192 (W.D. Wis. 1995).

S. W. and Joanne W. v. Holbrook Public Schools, 221 F. Supp.2d 222 (D. Mass. 2002).

Tony McCann, In re, 17 EHLR 551 (Tenn. Ct. App. 1990).

Trent N., In re, 569 N.W.2d 719 (Wis. Ct. App. 1997).

Underwood, J. K., & Mead, J. F. (1995). *Legal aspects of special education & pupil services.* Boston: Allyn & Bacon.

United States Code (U.S.C.), as cited.

Waechter v. School District No. 14–030 of Cassopolis, 773 F. Supp. 1005 (W.D. Mich. 1991).

Walpole Public Schools, 22 IDELR 1075 (SEA Mass. 1995).

Williams Letter, 21 IDELR 73 (OSEP 1994).

Wise v. Pea Ridge School District, 855 F.2d 560 (8th Cir. 1988).

7 Conclusions and Recommendations for Practice

┌─ **Key Concepts in This Chapter** ─────────────────────────

◆ Due Process Requirements

◆ Manifestation Determination

◆ Emergency Removals

INTRODUCTION

Students with disabilities, like all children, sometimes misbehave and require discipline. Under the Individuals with Disabilities Education Act (IDEA, 2006), students with disabilities continue to remain subject to disciplinary actions if they misbehave. However, unlike their peers who do not have disabilities, students with disabilities are entitled to additional due process protections when their behavior may result in their facing the substantial loss of educational opportunities. The extra steps are required because the IDEA confers rights on students with disabilities to a free appropriate public education (FAPE). Section 504 of the Rehabilitation Act (Rehabilitation Act, Section 504, 2006) and the Americans with Disabilities Act (2006) also provide protections for students with disabilities.

REQUIRED DUE PROCESS

Students with disabilities may be suspended for periods of up to 10 school days if school officials follow normal due process procedures. Educators may impose other common minor disciplinary sanctions such as in-school suspensions, detentions, or time-outs without resort to the IDEA's change in placement procedures. Conversely, when officials are contemplating expulsions or transfers of students to other educational settings, such as alternative schools, they must apply the IDEA's protections. Of paramount importance, educators must provide parents with proper notice of their intended actions and their rights in the process. Figure 7.1 provides an example of a notice that educators can send parents when their children face suspensions of 10 days or less. Figure 7.2 is a sample notice that educators should include if they are contemplating the imposition of expulsions or suspensions of more than 10 days.

Figure 7.1 Sample Suspension Hearing Notice

Notice to Parent Regarding Possible Suspension

[*Insert date*]

[*Insert parent's name*]

[*Insert address*]

[*Insert city, state, and zip code*]

Dear [*Insert parent's name*]:

An informal disciplinary hearing will convene regarding your child, [*insert student's name*], on [*insert date*], at [*insert time*] in the principal's office at the [*insert school name*]. The specific reasons for the disciplinary hearing are as follows:
[*briefly describe rule infraction or list student handbook violations*]
At the conclusion of the hearing, the hearing officer will determine what disciplinary action, if any, will be taken. One option may be a brief suspension. You are invited to attend the hearing. While the hearing will be informal, you and your child will be given the full opportunity to respond to the above complaints.

Your child has been classified as a student with disabilities. This means that the chair of your child's special education team has been informed of this action and has also been invited to attend the hearing. If you have any concerns about whether your child's educational program is adequately meeting your child's needs, you may discuss it with the special education team chair at that time.

A short-term suspension is considered to be a normal disciplinary action and requires only notification and the opportunity to be heard. However, if the total number of days of suspension exceeds 10 school days, we will provide additional due process safeguards. These procedures will include all of the due process safeguards your child is entitled to under the Individuals with Disabilities Education Act; these procedures are outlined in the enclosed notice.

Sincerely,

[*Signature of School Principal or Designee*]

Figure 7.2 Sample Notice of Rights Regarding Possible Long-Term Exclusion

**Notice of Rights to the Parent of a Student
With Disabilities Facing a Long-Term Suspension or Expulsion**

1. Students with disabilities have the right to have members of their individualized education program (IEP) teams, including the parents, along with other school personnel, determine whether the disciplinary code infraction was a manifestation of, or was related to, the students' disabilities or if the misbehavior resulted from improper implementation of an IEP.

2. If IEP teams determine that a manifestation exists or that an IEP was improperly implemented, children may not be expelled or suspended for more than 10 school days.

3. Any actions that IEP teams make may be appealed to an independent hearing officer. The hearing officer's decision may be appealed to a hearing review panel [in states so providing] and to the state or federal courts. Parents are entitled to expedited hearings to contest manifestation determinations if they disagree with the decisions of the IEP team. Expedited hearings must be conducted within 20 days, and decisions must be rendered within 10 days of the hearings.

4. If IEP teams determine that no relationship exists between students' conduct and their disabilities, the students may be expelled or suspended for more than 10 school days. Decisions to expel students are subject to the appeals process listed in #3 above. During any appeals, students remain expelled.

5. Students are entitled to receive special education and related services during disciplinary exclusions from school for more than 10 school days. Even if students are expelled, school boards must continue to provide special education services.

6. Until all due process proceedings are completed, students are to remain in the placements determined by school administrators. Students who are found to have possessed weapons, engaged in drug violations, or have inflicted serious bodily injury on others may be placed in alternative educational settings for periods of up to 45 days. If parents object to placements in interim alternative educational settings, they may request expedited hearings. Still, during the pendency of hearings, students must remain in the interim settings.

7. If students are removed from their educational settings for more than 10 school days or are placed in interim alternative educational settings, educators must conduct functional behavioral assessments (FBAs) and implement behavior intervention plans (BIPs) if they do not already exist. If BIPs are in place, they will be reviewed and revised if necessary.

MANIFESTATION DETERMINATION

When educators are contemplating a student expulsion, they must first determine whether the misconduct precipitating the disciplinary action was a manifestation of the student's disabilities. If the conduct was such a manifestation, then the student may not be expelled. This determination must be made within 10 school days of any decision to change a student's placement and by a committee composed of members of the student's IEP team in consultation with the student's parents. According to the IDEA, other qualified individuals may be included in making this decision; this approach allows school administrators who were not part of original IEP teams to participate in making the manifestation determination.

In making the manifestation determination, the manifestation review committee must evaluate whether the behavior in question was caused by or had a direct and substantial relationship to the student's disabilities or if it was the direct result of school personnel's failure to implement the student's IEP. If the review committee decides that the misconduct was not a manifestation of the student's disabilities, the student may be expelled. However, during expulsion periods, students must be provided with special education services. If the misconduct was a manifestation of the student's disabilities, the student may not be expelled. Even so, IEP teams can propose new educational placements if members agree that the current placements are not meeting students' needs. If the parents disagree with the results of manifestation determinations or any other actions taken by school personnel that impact the student's placement, parents may contest them via the IDEA's administrative due process mechanism. All hearings in this regard must be expedited.

EMERGENCY REMOVALS

The IDEA does allow the emergency removal of dangerous students with disabilities even when the misconduct stems from their disabilities. If students are accused of possessing weapons or drugs or of the infliction of serious bodily injuries on school property or at a school function, they may immediately be removed for 10 school days by following the normal suspension procedures. The students then may be placed in interim alternative placements for a 45-day period. These alternative placements must be ones that allow the students to progress in the general education curriculum and in which they can continue to receive special education services. In a major difference from the IDEA's standard due process procedures, students found guilty of drug, weapon, or infliction of serious bodily injury charges may be placed in interim alternative settings while due process hearings are pending even without parental agreement.

In situations not involving weapons, drugs, or the infliction of serious bodily injuries but where school personnel sense that students' continued presence in the school would cause a danger to others or could substantially interrupt the educational process, school administrators may obtain relief by way of judicial or hearing officer orders. Nonetheless, in order to obtain injunctions to prevent students from attending their former educational programs, school officials must show that they have done all they can to mitigate the danger or chance of disruption and that less restrictive alternatives are not feasible. As noted by the Supreme Court in *Honig v. Doe*, the burden of proof in this regard clearly is on school officials. Proper documentation of disciplinary infractions and the steps school personnel have taken to curb future misbehavior is essential. The *Specific Incident Report* form in Figure 7.3 and the *Discipline Record* form in Figure 7.4 can be used for this purpose.

Figure 7.3   Sample Incident Report Form

Specific Incident Report

Type of Incident:

____ Assault/Battery on a Student
____ Assault/Battery on a School Employee
____ Infliction of Serious Bodily Injury
____ Sexual Assault
____ Weapon Possession
____ Drug or Alcohol Possession
____ Drug or Alcohol Distribution
____ Theft
____ Destruction of Property
____ Harassment
____ Bullying
____ Civil Rights Violation
____ Other _____

Date and Time of Incident:

_____

School or Location:

_____

Names, Addresses, and Telephone Numbers of Students Involved:

_____

_____

_____

Names, Addresses, Telephone Numbers, and Positions/Titles of Witnesses:

_____

_____

_____

Narrative Description of Incident:

_____

_____

_____

(Continued)

Figure 7.3 (Continued)

Description of Immediate Action Taken:

_____

_____

_____

Planned Follow-up Action:

_____

_____

_____

Have the parents/guardians of the students involved been notified?

_____Yes _____No _____ By Telephone _____ By Letter _____ By Email

Was the incident reported to the police? _____Yes _____No

If yes, please provide pertinent information (name of investigating officer, file number, etc.):

_____

_____

_____

Was the incident reported to any other agency? _____Yes _____No

If yes, please provide pertinent information:

_____

_____

_____

Were the students provided an opportunity to present their versions of the incident?
_____Yes _____No

If yes, please provide pertinent details (you may attach other documents such as a hearing report):

_____

_____

_____

Name of Person Filing Report: _____

Position/Title: _____

Signature: _____

Date: _____

A copy of this report should be submitted to the superintendent of schools and the school district's director of security within one day of the incident. If any of the students involved were in special education programs, a copy should also be sent to the director of special education.

Figure 7.4 Sample Disciplinary Record Form

Discipline Record

Student: _____

Date	Disciplinary Code Infraction	Action Taken	Administrator

School officials also are required to conduct FBAs and develop BIPs at specified junctures during the disciplinary process. School personnel would be prudent to include these as part of the annual IEP process for all students with disabilities who have a history of misbehavior, even though the IDEA does not mandate such an action. Being proactive with students who have a propensity toward misconduct may save time and turmoil later on if misbehavior arises. If BIPs are included as part of students' IEPs and are agreed to by the parents in advance, they should lessen conflict between school officials and parents if disciplinary action becomes necessary, as long as the steps outlined in the plan were implemented. By the same token, hearing officers and judges are more likely to support school boards if school personnel followed previously agreed on BIPs.

Neither the IDEA nor its regulations specify what elements should be included in FBAs. Nevertheless, at a minimum FBAs should contain records of staff observations of the student that document aspects of the student's behavior; analysis of the situations that trigger misbehavior; analysis of the effectiveness of previous interventions; medical, psychological, and social data that could affect behavior; and any other information that could provide insight into the student's behavior.

At the same time, the IDEA and its regulations provide little guidance as to what elements should be included in BIPs. In fact, the IDEA does not even require written plans. Still, given the need for proper documentation if litigation stems from disciplinary action, school officials are advised to put all BIPs in writing. Plans should include strategies for dealing with students' behavior when it surfaces, along with long-term strategies for preventing future occurrences. BIPs also should include supports that school officials will provide to the students to help them deal with the situations that tend to precipitate the behavior. Finally, the BIPs should outline expected behaviors, delineate inappropriate conduct, and specify the positive and negative consequences for any behaviors. Figure 7.5 is a sample BIP.

Figure 7.5   Sample Behavior Intervention Plan

Behavior Intervention Plan

Student: _____   Date: _____

[*In the table below, list all those who participated in the development of the behavior intervention plan and their respective positions.*]

Participants	Position/Role

[*Insert student's name*]'s IEP team has determined that [*his/her*] disability may, on occasion, cause [*him/her*] to misbehave or in some way disrupt the educational process for others. Therefore, we have created a behavior intervention plan (BIP) for [*insert student's name*]. This BIP is an attachment to and is considered a part of [*insert student's name*]'s IEP. It will be reviewed whenever [*insert student's name*]'s IEP is reviewed.

[*Insert student's name*] is expected to conform to the terms of the BIP, and any and all infractions will be dealt with as outlined in the BIP. However, nothing in the BIP is intended to prevent school officials from taking such emergency or immediate steps as are necessary to restore order, maintain proper discipline, or otherwise prevent a dangerous situation from existing in the school.

[*Insert student's name*] has been placed in a special education program, and an IEP has been developed that is designed to reduce the effects of [*insert student's name*]'s disability and allow [*insert student's name*] to perform according to [*his/her*] potential. This program is designed to help [*insert student's name*] learn appropriate behavior through the use of behavior management techniques.

[*Insert student's name*] may not engage in any activity that will endanger [*himself/herself*], other students, or staff members. [*Insert student's name*] also may not engage in any behavior that will damage school property, the property of other students, or the property of staff members. Furthermore, [*insert student's name*] is not permitted to engage in activities that will substantially interfere with the educational process for other students. To these ends, [*insert student's name*] may not engage in any behavior that is prohibited by the student handbook, a copy of which is attached.

The following steps will be taken in the event of an infraction that substantially disrupts the educational environment for others:

1. The teacher will employ usual classroom disciplinary procedures.

2. If Step 1 fails to correct the misconduct, the teacher will seek assistance from the school adjustment counselor and/or a school administrator.

3. If the misconduct continues, [*insert student's name*] may be removed from the classroom and temporarily detained in a time-out area.

4. If the misconduct continues, [*insert student's name*] may be placed on an in-school suspension. Special education services will be provided in the in-school suspension room, and the student will be expected to complete all assignments.

5. If the misconduct continues when [*insert student's name*] returns to class, [*insert student's name*] may be suspended for 3 to 5 days; during the suspension period [*insert student's name*] will be expected to complete all school assignments as provided by teachers and special education staff.

6. If [*insert student's name*] is suspended for a cumulative total of 10 school days in any school year, the IEP team will reconvene within 5 days of the imposition of the suspension that exceeds the 10 cumulative days to review this BIP, determine if a more restrictive placement may be necessary, or develop some other appropriate alternative plan of action to curb the disruption.

The following steps will be taken in the event of an infraction that presents a threat to the safety of the student, other students, or staff:

1. [*Insert student's name*] will be removed from the situation immediately.

2. An informal due process hearing will be held to determine if there is just cause for a suspension.

3. The IEP team will be convened to determine if [*insert student's name*]'s misbehavior is causally related to his or her disability or is due to an inappropriate placement.

4a. If the IEP team determines that the misbehavior is a manifestation of [*insert student's name*]'s disability, the team will determine if [*his/her*] current IEP is sufficient to meet [*his/her*] needs; if not, the IEP will be revised.

4b. If the team finds that the misbehavior is the result of an inappropriate placement, [*insert student's name*]'s placement will be reviewed and revised.

5. If [*insert student's name*] is suspended for a cumulative total of 10 school days in one school year, the IEP team will reconvene within 5 days of the imposition of the suspension that exceeds the 10 cumulative days to consider whether a more restrictive placement may be necessary or to develop some other appropriate alternative plan of action to curb the dangerous behavior.

In order to assist [*insert student's name*] in managing [*his/her*] behavior and to teach [*him/her*] appropriate behavior, we will employ the following strategies:

1. [*Insert student's name*]'s teacher will record, by making a check mark on a chart, every 15-minute period of class time in which [*insert student's name*] follows all class rules, is on-task, and behaves appropriately.

2. [*Insert student's name*] will be allowed to go to the computer lab to use educational game software as a reward for appropriate behavior. [*Insert student's name*] may exchange 12 check marks for 15 minutes in the lab.

3. If [*insert student's name*] thinks that [*he/she*] is "losing control," [*he/she*] may signal the teacher and will be allowed to go to the assistant principal's office for a voluntary time-out. [*Insert student's name*] may return to class when [*he/she*] feels [*he/she*] has regained control.

(Continued)

Figure 7.5 (Continued)

4. If [*insert student's name*] becomes disruptive and the teacher is unable to calm [*him/her*] down within a few minutes, [*he/she*] will be required to go to the assistant principal's office for an involuntary time-out. [*Insert student's name*] may return to class at the assistant principal's discretion when [*insert student's name*] shows that [*he/she*] has regained control. All time spent in an involuntary time-out must be made up either during recess or after school.

5. [*Insert student's name*] will be provided with twice-weekly guidance counseling sessions to help [*him/her*] learn to manage stress. During these sessions the counselor will discuss the situations that led to a time-out and alternatives to disruptive conduct.

6. The guidance counselor will also be available for crisis resolution sessions when necessary.

7. The teacher will implement a conflict resolution curriculum in the classroom.

8. The teacher will be provided with consultation on a weekly basis with a behavior specialist to develop appropriate classroom management techniques for dealing with [*insert student's name*].

9. The behavior specialist will consult with [*insert student's name*]'s parents on a weekly basis to teach them the behavior techniques and strategies that will be used in the classroom. Consistency between the classroom and the home environment is important in teaching [*insert student's name*] appropriate behavior and to control [*his/her*] own behavior. Therefore, it is important for [*insert student's name*]'s parent[s] to use those same techniques and strategies at home.

10. A daily progress report will be sent home to facilitate communication with parents. This report will record [*insert student's name*]'s behavior and effort for each period during the day. Parents should sign this report to show that they have seen it and return it to school the following day.

11. Conferences will be held on a monthly basis with parents to discuss [*Insert student's name*]'s progress.

I accept the above behavior intervention plan and agree that it will be attached to and become part of the IEP covering the period _____ to _____.

Parent's Signature: _____

Date: _____

SUMMARY

The administration of disciplinary sanctions for students with disabilities has been one of the more contentious aspects of the IDEA. It is a complex issue, because it counters the ever-present duty of school officials to maintain order, discipline, and a safe educational environment against the entitlement students with disabilities have to a free appropriate public education in the least restrictive environment. The current provisions of the IDEA, along with existing case law, strike an appropriate balance. School officials may take disciplinary action against students with disabilities. Still, in taking disciplinary action, school administrators must follow the IDEA's more stringent procedures. This allows misbehaving students to be disciplined but also removes the possibility that they will be deprived of their right to a free appropriate public education for behavior that stems from their disabilities. Figure 7.6 provides a summary and timeline for the procedural steps that must be followed when disciplining students with disabilities.

Figure 7.6 Procedural Steps and Timelines in the Disciplinary Process

When students with disabilities misbehave, educators should take the following steps (time limitations are in parentheses):

- Take whatever measures are necessary to restore order and maintain discipline (immediately).
- Suspend students (for up to 10 school days) by following normal procedures.
- Conduct FBAs and develop BIPs if these are not already in place; review the FBAs and BIPs if they are in place (within 10 school days).
- If expulsion is under consideration, complete manifestation determinations (within 10 school days).
    - o If officials determine that students' misconduct was a manifestation of their disabilities, the children may not be expelled but may be moved to more restrictive placements by following the IDEA's change in placement procedures.
    - o If officials decide that there is no relationship between student disabilities and misconduct, the children may be expelled, but they must continue to receive special education services during the expulsion period.
- If students' misconduct involved weapons, drugs, or the infliction of serious bodily injuries, consider placing offenders in interim alternative educational settings (for up to 45 school days).
- If school personnel are of the opinion that maintaining students' current placements is likely to result in injuries to the students or others, seek hearing officer or judicial orders to change the students' placements (immediately) if they are not expelled or moved to interim alternative educational settings.
- At the end of expulsion periods or interim alternative placements, either return students to their former placements or develop new placements by following the IDEA's change in placement procedures.

REFERENCES

Americans with Disabilities Act, 42 U.S.C. §§ 12101–12213 (2006).
Honig v. Doe, 484 U.S. 305 (1988).
Individuals with Disabilities Education Act (IDEA), 20 U.S.C. §§ 1400–1482 (2006).
Rehabilitation Act, Section 504, 29 U.S.C. § 794 (2006).

Resource A

Provisions of the IDEA Relevant to Discipline

20 U.S.C. § 1412 State Eligibility

(a) In general

A State is eligible for assistance under this subchapter for a fiscal year if the State submits a plan that provides assurances to the Secretary that the State has in effect policies and procedures to ensure that the State meets each of the following conditions:

(1) Free appropriate public education

(A) In general

A free appropriate public education is available to all children with disabilities residing in the State between the ages of 3 and 21, inclusive, including children with disabilities who have been suspended or expelled from school.

20 U.S.C. § 1415 Procedural Safeguards

(b) Placement in alternative educational setting

(1) Authority of school personnel

(A) Case-by-case determination

School personnel may consider any unique circumstances on a case-by-case basis when determining whether to order a change in placement for a child with a disability who violates a code of student conduct.

(B) Authority

School personnel under this subsection may remove a child with a disability who violates a code of student conduct from their current placement to an appropriate interim alternative educational setting, another setting, or suspension, for not more than 10 school days (to the extent such alternatives are applied to children without disabilities).

(C) Additional authority

If school personnel seek to order a change in placement that would exceed 10 school days and the behavior that gave rise to the violation of the school code is determined not to be a manifestation of the child's disability pursuant to subparagraph (E), the relevant disciplinary procedures applicable to children without disabilities may be applied to the child in the same manner and for the same duration in which the procedures would be applied to children without disabilities, except as provided in section 1412(a)(1) of this title although it may be provided in an interim alternative educational setting.

(D) Services

A child with a disability who is removed from the child's current placement under subparagraph (G) (irrespective of whether the behavior is determined to be a manifestation of the child's disability) or subparagraph (C) shall—

(i) continue to receive educational services, as provided in section 1412(a)(1) of this title, so as to enable the child to continue to participate in the general education curriculum, although in another setting, and to progress toward meeting the goals set out in the child's IEP; and

(ii) receive, as appropriate, a functional behavioral assessment, behavioral intervention services and modifications, that are designed to address the behavior violation so that it does not recur.

(E) Manifestation determination

(i) In general

Except as provided in subparagraph (B), within 10 school days of any decision to change the placement of a child with a disability because of a violation of a code of student conduct, the local educational agency, the parent, and relevant members of the IEP Team (as determined by the parent and the local educational agency) shall review all relevant information in the student's file, including the child' s IEP, any teacher observations, and any relevant information provided by the parents to determine—

(I) if the conduct in question was caused by, or had a direct and substantial relationship to, the child's disability; or

(II) if the conduct in question was the direct result of the local educational agency's failure to implement the IEP.

(ii) Manifestation

If the local educational agency, the parent, and relevant members of the IEP Team determine that either subclause (I) or (II) of clause (i) is applicable for the child, the conduct shall be determined to be a manifestation of the child's disability.

(F) Determination that behavior was a manifestation

If the local educational agency, the parent, and relevant members of the IEP Team make the determination that the conduct was a manifestation of the child's disability, the IEP Team shall—

(i) conduct a functional behavioral assessment, and implement a behavioral intervention plan for such child, provided that the local educational agency had not conducted such assessment prior to such determination before the behavior that resulted in a change in placement described in subparagraph (C) or (G);

(ii) in the situation where a behavioral intervention plan has been developed, review the behavioral intervention plan if the child already has such a behavioral intervention plan, and modify it, as necessary, to address the behavior; and

(iii) except as provided in subparagraph (G), return the child to the placement from which the child was removed, unless the parent and the local educational agency agree to a change of placement as part of the modification of the behavioral intervention plan.

(G) Special circumstances

School personnel may remove a student to an interim alternative educational setting for not more than 45 school days without regard to whether the behavior is determined to be a manifestation of the child's disability, in cases where a child—

(i) carries or possesses a weapon to or at school, on school premises, or to or at a school function under the jurisdiction of a State or local educational agency;

(ii) knowingly possesses or uses illegal drugs, or sells or solicits the sale of a controlled substance, while at school, on school premises, or at a school function under the jurisdiction of a State or local educational agency; or

(iii) has inflicted serious bodily injury upon another person while at school, on school premises, or at a school function under the jurisdiction of a State or local educational agency.

(H) Notification

Not later than the date on which the decision to take disciplinary action is made, the local educational agency shall notify the parents of that decision, and of all procedural safeguards accorded under this section.

(2) Determination of setting

The interim alternative educational setting in subparagraphs (C) and (G) of paragraph (1) shall be determined by the IEP Team.

(3) Appeal

(A) In general

The parent of a child with a disability who disagrees with any decision regarding placement, or the manifestation determination under this subsection, or a local educational agency that believes that maintaining the current placement of the child is substantially likely to result in injury to the child or to others, may request a hearing.

(B) Authority of hearing officer

(i) In general

A hearing officer shall hear, and make a determination regarding, an appeal requested under subparagraph (A).

(ii) Change of placement order

In making the determination under clause (i), the hearing officer may order a change in placement of a child with a disability. In such situations, the hearing officer may—

(I) return a child with a disability to the placement from which the child was removed; or

(II) order a change in placement of a child with a disability to an appropriate interim alternative educational setting for not more than 45 school days if the hearing officer determines that maintaining the current placement of such child is substantially likely to result in injury to the child or to others.

(4) Placement during appeals

When an appeal under paragraph (3) has been requested by either the parent or the local educational agency—

(A) the child shall remain in the interim alternative educational setting pending the decision of the hearing officer or until the expiration of the time period provided for in paragraph (1)(C), whichever occurs first, unless the parent and the State or local educational agency agree otherwise; and

(B) the State or local educational agency shall arrange for an expedited hearing, which shall occur within 20 school days of the date the hearing is requested and shall result in a determination within 10 school days after the hearing.

(5) Protections for children not yet eligible for special education and related services

(A) In general

A child who has not been determined to be eligible for special education and related services under this subchapter and who has engaged in behavior that violates a code of student conduct, may assert any of the protections provided for in this subchapter if the local educational agency had knowledge (as determined in accordance with this paragraph) that the child was a child with a disability before the behavior that precipitated the disciplinary action occurred.

(B) Basis of knowledge

A local educational agency shall be deemed to have knowledge that a child is a child with a disability if, before the behavior that precipitated the disciplinary action occurred—

(i) the parent of the child has expressed concern in writing to supervisory or administrative personnel of the appropriate educational agency, or a teacher of the child, that the child is in need of special education and related services;

(ii) the parent of the child has requested an evaluation of the child pursuant to section 1414(a)(1)(B) of this title; or

(iii) the teacher of the child, or other personnel of the local educational agency, has expressed specific concerns about a pattern of behavior demonstrated by the child directly to the director of special education of such agency or to other supervisory personnel of the agency.

(C) Exception

A local educational agency shall not be deemed to have knowledge that the child is a child with a disability if the parent of the child has not allowed an evaluation of the child pursuant to section 1414 of this title or has refused services under this subchapter or the child has been evaluated and it was determined that the child was not a child with a disability under this subchapter.

(D) Conditions that apply if no basis of knowledge

(i) In general

If a local educational agency does not have knowledge that a child is a child with a disability (in accordance with subparagraph (B) or (C)) prior to taking disciplinary measures against the child, the child may be subjected to disciplinary measures applied to children without disabilities who engaged in comparable behaviors consistent with clause (ii).

(ii) Limitations

If a request is made for an evaluation of a child during the time period in which the child is subjected to disciplinary measures under this subsection, the evaluation shall be conducted in an expedited manner. If the child is determined to be a child with a disability, taking into consideration information from the evaluation conducted by the agency and information provided by the parents, the agency shall provide special education and related services in accordance with this subchapter, except that, pending the results of the evaluation, the child shall remain in the educational placement determined by school authorities.

(6) Referral to and action by law enforcement and judicial authorities

(A) Rule of construction

Nothing in this subchapter shall be construed to prohibit an agency from reporting a crime committed by a child with a disability to appropriate authorities or to prevent State law enforcement and judicial authorities from exercising their responsibilities with regard to the application of Federal and State law to crimes committed by a child with a disability.

(B) Transmittal of records

An agency reporting a crime committed by a child with a disability shall ensure that copies of the special education and disciplinary records of the child are transmitted for consideration by the appropriate authorities to whom the agency reports the crime.

(7) Definitions

In this subsection:

(A) Controlled substance

The term "controlled substance" means a drug or other substance identified under schedule I, II, III, IV, or V in section 812(c) of Title 21.

(B) Illegal drug

The term "illegal drug" means a controlled substance but does not include a controlled substance that is legally possessed or used under the supervision of a licensed healthcare professional or that is legally possessed or used under any other authority under that Act or under any other provision of Federal law.

(C) Weapon

The term "weapon" has the meaning given the term "dangerous weapon" under section 930(g)(2) of Title 18.

(D) Serious bodily injury

The term "serious bodily injury" has the meaning given the term "serious bodily injury" under paragraph (3) of subsection (h) of section 1365 of Title 18.

Resource B

*IDEA Regulations
Relevant to Discipline*

DISCIPLINE PROCEDURES

§300.530 Authority of school personnel.

(a) Case-by-case determination. School personnel may consider any unique circumstances on a case-by-case basis when determining whether a change in placement, consistent with the other requirements of this section, is appropriate for a child with a disability who violates a code of student conduct.

(b) General.

(1) School personnel under this section may remove a child with a disability who violates a code of student conduct from his or her current placement to an appropriate interim alternative educational setting, another setting, or suspension, for not more than 10 consecutive school days (to the extent those alternatives are applied to children without disabilities), and for additional removals of not more than 10 consecutive school days in that same school year for separate incidents of misconduct (as long as those removals do not constitute a change of placement under §300.536).

(2) After a child with a disability has been removed from his or her current placement for 10 school days in the same school year, during any subsequent days of removal the public agency must provide services to the extent required under paragraph (d) of this section.

(c) Additional authority. For disciplinary changes in placement that would exceed 10 consecutive school days, if the behavior that gave rise to the violation of the school code is determined not to be a manifestation of the child's disability pursuant to paragraph (e) of this section, school personnel may apply the relevant disciplinary procedures to children with disabilities in the same manner and for the same duration as the procedures would be applied to children without disabilities, except as provided in paragraph (d) of this section.

(d) Services.

    (1) A child with a disability who is removed from the child's current placement pursuant to paragraphs (c) or (g) of this section must—

        (i) Continue to receive educational services, as provided in §300.101(a), so as to enable the child to continue to participate in the general education curriculum, although in another setting, and to progress toward meeting the goals set out in the child's IEP; and

        (ii) Receive, as appropriate, a functional behavioral assessment, and behavioral intervention services and modifications, that are designed to address the behavior violation so that it does not recur.

    (2) The services required by paragraph (d)(1), (d)(3), (d)(4), and (d)(5) of this section may be provided in an interim alternative educational setting.

    (3) A public agency is only required to provide services during periods of removal to a child with a disability who has been removed from his or her current placement for 10 school days or less in that school year, if it provides services to a child without disabilities who is similarly removed.

    (4) After a child with a disability has been removed from his or her current placement for 10 school days in the same school year, if the current removal is for not more than 10 consecutive school days and is not a change of placement under §300.536, school personnel, in consultation with at least one of the child's teachers, determine the extent to which services are needed, as provided in §300.101(a), so as to enable the child to continue to participate in the general education curriculum, although in another setting, and to progress toward meeting the goals set out in the child's IEP.

    (5) If the removal is a change of placement under §300.536, the child's IEP Team determines appropriate services under paragraph (d)(1) of this section.

(e) Manifestation determination.

    (1) Within 10 school days of any decision to change the placement of a child with a disability because of a violation of a code of student conduct, the LEA, the parent, and relevant members of the child's IEP Team (as determined by the parent and the LEA) must review all relevant information in the student's file, including the child's IEP, any teacher observations, and any relevant information provided by the parents to determine—

        (i) If the conduct in question was caused by, or had a direct and substantial relationship to, the child's disability; or

        (ii) If the conduct in question was the direct result of the LEA's failure to implement the IEP.

    (2) The conduct must be determined to be a manifestation of the child's disability if the LEA, the parent, and relevant members of the child's IEP Team determine that a condition in either paragraph (e)(1)(i) or (1)(ii) of this section was met.

    (3) If the LEA, the parent, and relevant members of the child's IEP Team determine the condition described in paragraph (e)(1)(ii) of this section was met, the LEA must take immediate steps to remedy those deficiencies.

(f) Determination that behavior was a manifestation. If the LEA, the parent, and relevant members of the IEP Team make the determination that the conduct was a manifestation of the child's disability, the IEP Team must—

    (1) Either—

        (i) Conduct a functional behavioral assessment, unless the LEA had conducted a functional behavioral assessment before the behavior that resulted in the change of placement occurred, and implement a behavioral intervention plan for the child; or

        (ii) If a behavioral intervention plan already has been developed, review the behavioral intervention plan, and modify it, as necessary, to address the behavior; and

    (2) Except as provided in paragraph (g) of this section, return the child to the placement from which the child was removed, unless the parent and the LEA agree to a change of placement as part of the modification of the behavioral intervention plan.

(g) Special circumstances. School personnel may remove a student to an interim alternative educational setting for not more than 45 school days without regard to whether the behavior is determined to be a manifestation of the child's disability, if the child—

   (1) Carries a weapon to or possesses a weapon at school, on school premises, or to or at a school function under the jurisdiction of an SEA or an LEA;

   (2) Knowingly possesses or uses illegal drugs, or sells or solicits the sale of a controlled substance, while at school, on school premises, or at a school function under the jurisdiction of an SEA or an LEA; or

   (3) Has inflicted serious bodily injury upon another person while at school, on school premises, or at a school function under the jurisdiction of an SEA or an LEA.

(h) Notification. On the date on which the decision is made to make a removal that constitutes a change of placement of a child with a disability because of a violation of a code of student conduct, the LEA must notify the parents of that decision, and provide the parents the procedural safeguards notice described in §300.504.

(i) Definitions. For purposes of this section, the following definitions apply:

   (1) Controlled substance means a drug or other substance identified under schedules I, II, III, IV, or V in section 202(c) of the Controlled Substances Act (21 U.S.C. 812(c)).

   (2) Illegal drug means a controlled substance; but does not include a controlled substance that is legally possessed or used under the supervision of a licensed health-care professional or that is legally possessed or used under any other authority under that Act or under any other provision of Federal law.

   (3) Serious bodily injury has the meaning given the term "serious bodily injury" under paragraph (3) of subsection (h) of section 1365 of Title 18, United States Code.

   (4) Weapon has the meaning given the term "dangerous weapon" under paragraph (2) of the first subsection (g) of section 930 of Title 18, United States Code.

(Authority: 20 U.S.C. 1415(k)(1) and (7))

§300.531 Determination of setting.

The child's IEP Team determines the interim alternative educational setting for services under §300.530(c), (d)(5), and (g).
(Authority: 20 U.S.C. 1415(k)(2))

§300.532 Appeal.

(a) General. The parent of a child with a disability who disagrees with any decision regarding placement under §§300.530 and 300.531, or the manifestation determination under §300.530(e), or an LEA that believes that maintaining the current placement of the child is substantially likely to result in injury to the child or others, may appeal the decision by requesting a hearing. The hearing is requested by filing a complaint pursuant to §§300.507 and 300.508(a) and (b).

(b) Authority of hearing officer.

    (1) A hearing officer under §300.511 hears and makes a determination regarding an appeal under paragraph (a) of this section.

    (2) In making the determination under paragraph (b)(1) of this section, the hearing officer may—

        (i) Return the child with a disability to the placement from which the child was removed if the hearing officer determines that the removal was a violation of §300.530 or that the child's behavior was a manifestation of the child's disability; or

        (ii) Order a change of placement of the child with a disability to an appropriate interim alternative educational setting for not more than 45 school days if the hearing officer determines that maintaining the current placement of the child is substantially likely to result in injury to the child or to others.

    (3) The procedures under paragraphs (a) and (b)(1) and (2) of this section may be repeated, if the LEA believes that returning the child to the original placement is substantially likely to result in injury to the child or to others.

(c) Expedited due process hearing.

    (1) Whenever a hearing is requested under paragraph (a) of this section, the parents or the LEA involved in the dispute must have an opportunity for an impartial due process hearing consistent with the requirements of §§300.507 and 300.508(a)

through (c) and §§300.510 through 300.514, except as provided in paragraph (c)(2) through (4) of this section.

(2) The SEA or LEA is responsible for arranging the expedited due process hearing, which must occur within 20 school days of the date the complaint requesting the hearing is filed. The hearing officer must make a determination within 10 school days after the hearing.

(3) Unless the parents and LEA agree in writing to waive the resolution meeting described in paragraph (c)(3)(i) of this section, or agree to use the mediation process described in §300.506—

(i) A resolution meeting must occur within seven days of receiving notice of the due process complaint; and

(ii) The due process hearing may proceed unless the matter has been resolved to the satisfaction of both parties within 15 days of the receipt of the due process complaint.

(4) A State may establish different State-imposed procedural rules for expedited due process hearings conducted under this section than it has established for other due process hearings, but, except for the timelines as modified in paragraph (c)(3) of this section, the State must ensure that the requirements in §§300.510 through 300.514 are met.

(5) The decisions on expedited due process hearings are appealable consistent with §300.514.

(Authority: 20 U.S.C. 1415(k)(3) and (4)(B), 1415(f)(1)(A))

§300.533 Placement during appeals.

When an appeal under §300.532 has been made by either the parent or the LEA, the child must remain in the interim alternative educational setting pending the decision of the hearing officer or until the expiration of the time period specified in §300.530(c) or (g), whichever occurs first, unless the parent and the SEA or LEA agree otherwise.

(Authority: 20 U.S.C. 1415(k)(4)(A))

§300.534 Protections for children not determined eligible for special education and related services.

(a) General. A child who has not been determined to be eligible for special education and related services under this part and who has engaged in behavior that violated a code of student conduct may assert any of the protections provided for in this part if the public agency had knowledge (as determined in accordance with paragraph (b) of this section) that the child was a child with a disability before the behavior that precipitated the disciplinary action occurred.

(b) Basis of knowledge. A public agency must be deemed to have knowledge that a child is a child with a disability if before the behavior that precipitated the disciplinary action occurred—

(1) The parent of the child expressed concern in writing to supervisory or administrative personnel of the appropriate educational agency, or a teacher of the child, that the child is in need of special education and related services;

(2) The parent of the child requested an evaluation of the child pursuant to §§300.300 through 300.311; or

(3) The teacher of the child, or other personnel of the LEA, expressed specific concerns about a pattern of behavior demonstrated by the child directly to the director of special education of the agency or to other supervisory personnel of the agency.

(c) Exception. A public agency would not be deemed to have knowledge under paragraph (b) of this section if—

(1) The parent of the child—

(i) Has not allowed an evaluation of the child pursuant to §§300.300 through 300.311; or
(ii) Has refused services under this part; or

(2) The child has been evaluated in accordance with §§300.300 through 300.311 and determined to not be a child with a disability under this part.

(d) Conditions that apply if no basis of knowledge.

(1) If a public agency does not have knowledge that a child is a child with a disability (in accordance with paragraphs (b) and (c) of this section) prior to taking disciplinary measures against the child, the child may be subjected to the disciplinary measures applied to children without disabilities who engage in comparable behaviors consistent with paragraph (d)(2) of this section.

(2)

(i) If a request is made for an evaluation of a child during the time period in which the child is subjected to disciplinary measures under §300.530, the evaluation must be conducted in an expedited manner.
(ii) Until the evaluation is completed, the child remains in the educational placement determined by school authorities,

which can include suspension or expulsion without educational services.

   (iii) If the child is determined to be a child with a disability, taking into consideration information from the evaluation conducted by the agency and information provided by the parents, the agency must provide special education and related services in accordance with this part, including the requirements of §§300.530 through 300.536 and section 612(a)(1)(A) of the Act.

(Authority: 20 U.S.C. 1415(k)(5))

§300.535 Referral to and action by law enforcement and judicial authorities.

(a) Rule of construction. Nothing in this part prohibits an agency from reporting a crime committed by a child with a disability to appropriate authorities or prevents State law enforcement and judicial authorities from exercising their responsibilities with regard to the application of Federal and State law to crimes committed by a child with a disability.

(b) Transmittal of records.

   (1) An agency reporting a crime committed by a child with a disability must ensure that copies of the special education and disciplinary records of the child are transmitted for consideration by the appropriate authorities to whom the agency reports the crime.

   (2) An agency reporting a crime under this section may transmit copies of the child's special education and disciplinary records only to the extent that the transmission is permitted by the Family Educational Rights and Privacy Act.

(Authority: 20 U.S.C. 1415(k)(6))

§300.536 Change of placement because of disciplinary removals.

(a) For purposes of removals of a child with a disability from the child's current educational placement under §§300.530 through 300.535, a change of placement occurs if—

   (1) The removal is for more than 10 consecutive school days; or

(2) The child has been subjected to a series of removals that constitute a pattern—

    (i) Because the series of removals total more than 10 school days in a school year;

    (ii) Because the child's behavior is substantially similar to the child's behavior in previous incidents that resulted in the series of removals; and

    (iii) Because of such additional factors as the length of each removal, the total amount of time the child has been removed, and the proximity of the removals to one another.

(b)

(1) The public agency determines on a case-by-case basis whether a pattern of removals constitutes a change of placement.

(2) This determination is subject to review through due process and judicial proceedings.

(Authority: 20 U.S.C. 1415(k))

§300.537 State enforcement mechanisms.

Notwithstanding §§300.506(b)(7) and 300.510(d)(2), which provide for judicial enforcement of a written agreement reached as a result of mediation or a resolution meeting, there is nothing in this part that would prevent the SEA from using other mechanisms to seek enforcement of that agreement, provided that use of those mechanisms is not mandatory and does not delay or deny a party the right to seek enforcement of the written agreement in a State court of competent jurisdiction or in a district court of the United States.

(Authority: 20 U.S.C. 1415(e)(2)(F), 1415(f)(1)(B))

Resource C

HONIG

v.

DOE

Supreme Court of the United States, 1988

484 U.S. 305

Justice Brennan delivered the opinion of the Court.

As a condition of federal financial assistance, the Education of the Handicapped Act requires States to ensure a free appropriate public education for all disabled children within their jurisdictions. In aid of this goal, the Act establishes a comprehensive system of procedural safeguards . . . Among these safeguards is the so-called stay-put provision, which directs that a disabled child shall remain in [his or her] then current educational placement pending completion of any review proceedings, unless the parents and state or local educational agencies otherwise agree. Today we must decide whether, in the face of this statutory proscription, state or local school authorities may nevertheless unilaterally exclude disabled children from the classroom for dangerous or disruptive conduct growing out of their disabilities. . . .

I

. . . The present dispute grows out of the efforts of certain officials of the San Francisco Unified School District (SFUSD) to expel two emotionally disturbed children from school indefinitely for violent and disruptive conduct related to their disabilities. In November 1980, respondent John Doe assaulted another student at the Louise Lombard School, a developmental center for disabled children. Doe's April 1980 IEP identified him as a socially and physically awkward 17-year-old who experienced considerable difficulty controlling his impulses and anger. Among the goals set out in his IEP was improvement in [his] ability to relate to [his] peers [and to] cope with frustrating situations without resorting to aggressive acts. Frustrating situations, however, were an unfortunately prominent feature of Doe's school career: physical abnormalities, speech difficulties, and poor grooming habits had made him the target of teasing and ridicule as early as the

(Continued)

(Continued)

first grade; his 1980 IEP reflected his continuing difficulties with peers, noting that his social skills had deteriorated and that he could tolerate only minor frustration before exploding.

On November 6, 1980, Doe responded to the taunts of a fellow student in precisely the explosive manner anticipated by his IEP: he choked the student with sufficient force to leave abrasions on the child's neck, and kicked out a school window while being escorted to the principal's office afterwards. Doe admitted his misconduct and the school subsequently suspended him for five days. Thereafter, his principal referred the matter to the SFUSD Student Placement Committee (SPC or Committee) with the recommendation that Doe be expelled. On the day the suspension was to end, the SPC notified Doe's mother that it was proposing to exclude her child permanently from SFUSD and was therefore extending his suspension until such time as the expulsion proceedings were completed. The Committee further advised her that she was entitled to attend the November 25 hearing at which it planned to discuss the proposed expulsion.

After unsuccessfully protesting these actions by letter, Doe brought this suit... alleging that the suspension and proposed expulsion violated the EHA, he sought a temporary restraining order canceling the SPC hearing and requiring school officials to convene an IEP meeting. The District Judge granted the requested injunctive relief and further ordered defendants to provide home tutoring for Doe on an interim basis; shortly thereafter, she issued a preliminary injunction directing defendants to return Doe to his then current educational placement at Louise Lombard School pending completion of the IEP review process. Doe reentered school on December 15, 5½ weeks, and 24 school-days, after his initial suspension.

Respondent Jack Smith was identified as an emotionally disturbed child by the time he entered the second grade in 1976. School records prepared that year indicated that he was unable to control verbal or physical outburst[s] and exhibited a severe disturbance in relationships with peers and adults. Further evaluations subsequently revealed that he had been physically and emotionally abused as an infant and young child and that, despite above average intelligence, he experienced academic and social difficulties as a result of extreme hyperactivity and low self-esteem. Of particular concern was Smith's propensity for verbal hostility; one evaluator noted that the child reacted to stress by attempt[ing] to cover his feelings of low self worth through aggressive behavior... primarily verbal provocations.

Based on these evaluations, SFUSD placed Smith in a learning center for emotionally disturbed children. His grandparents, however, believed that his needs would be better served in the public school setting and, in September 1979, the school district acceded to their requests and enrolled him at A. P. Giannini Middle School. His February 1980 IEP recommended placement in a Learning Disability Group, stressing the need for close supervision and a highly structured environment. Like earlier evaluations, the February 1980 IEP noted that Smith was easily distracted, impulsive, and anxious; it therefore proposed a half-day schedule and suggested that the placement be undertaken on a trial basis.

At the beginning of the next school year, Smith was assigned to a full-day program; almost immediately thereafter he began misbehaving. School officials met twice with his grandparents in October 1980 to discuss returning him to a half-day program; although the grandparents agreed to the reduction, they apparently were never apprised of their right to challenge the decision through EHA procedures. The school officials also warned them that if the child continued his disruptive behavior—which included stealing, extorting money from fellow students, and making sexual comments to female classmates—they would seek to expel him. On November 14, they made good on this threat, suspending Smith for five days after he made further lewd comments. His principal referred the matter to the SPC, which recommended exclusion from SFUSD. As it did in John Doe's case, the Committee scheduled a hearing and extended the suspension indefinitely pending a final disposition in the matter. On November 28, Smith's counsel protested these actions on grounds essentially identical to those raised by Doe, and the SPC agreed to cancel the hearing and to return Smith to a half-day program at A. P. Giannini or to provide home tutoring. Smith's grandparents chose the latter option and the school began home instruction on December 10; on January 6, 1981, an IEP team convened to discuss alternative placements.

After learning of Doe's action, Smith sought and obtained leave to intervene in the suit. The District Court subsequently entered summary judgment in favor of respondents on their EHA claims and issued a permanent injunction. In a series of decisions, the District Judge found that the proposed expulsions and indefinite suspensions of respondents for conduct attributable to their disabilities deprived them of their congressionally mandated right to a free appropriate public education, as well as their right to have that education provided in accordance with the procedures set out in the EHA. The District Judge therefore permanently enjoined ... any disciplinary action other than a 2- or 5-day suspension against any disabled child for disability-related misconduct, or from effecting any other change in the educational placement of any such child without parental consent pending completion of any EHA proceedings. In addition, the judge barred the State from authorizing unilateral placement changes and directed it to establish an EHA compliance-monitoring system or, alternatively, to enact guidelines governing local school responses to disability-related misconduct. Finally, the judge ordered the State to provide services directly to disabled children when, in any individual case, the State determined that the local educational agency was unable or unwilling to do so.

... the Ninth Circuit affirmed the orders with slight modifications. Agreeing with the District Court that an indefinite suspension in aid of expulsion constitutes a prohibited change in placement under [the EHA], the Court of Appeals held that the stay-put provision admitted of no dangerousness exception and that the statute therefore rendered invalid those provisions of the California Education Code permitting the indefinite suspension or expulsion of disabled children for misconduct arising out of their disabilities. The court concluded, however, that fixed suspensions of up to 30 school days did not fall within the reach of [the EHA], and therefore upheld recent amendments to the state Education Code authorizing such suspensions. . . .

Petitioner Bill Honig, California Superintendent of Public Instruction, sought review in this Court, claiming that the Court of Appeals construction of the stay-put provision conflicted with that of several other Courts of Appeals which had recognized a dangerousness exception. . . . We granted certiorari to resolve these questions and now affirm.

II

. . .

III

The language of [the EHA] is unequivocal. It states plainly that during the pendency of any proceedings initiated under the Act, unless the state or local educational agency and the parents or guardian of a disabled child otherwise agree, the child *shall* remain in the

(Continued)

(Continued)

then current educational placement (emphasis added). Faced with this clear directive, petitioner asks us to read a dangerousness exception into the stay-put provision on the basis of either of two essentially inconsistent assumptions: first, that Congress thought the residual authority of school officials to exclude dangerous students from the classroom too obvious for comment; or second, that Congress inadvertently failed to provide such authority and this Court must therefore remedy the oversight. Because we cannot accept either premise, we decline petitioner's invitation to rewrite the statute.

Petitioner's arguments proceed, he suggests, from a simple, commonsense proposition: Congress could not have intended the stay-put provision to be read literally, for such a construction leads to the clearly unintended, and untenable, result that school districts must return violent or dangerous students to school while the often lengthy EHA proceedings run their course. We think it clear, however, that Congress very much meant to strip schools of the *unilateral* authority they had traditionally employed to exclude disabled students, particularly emotionally disturbed students, from school. In so doing, Congress did not leave school administrators powerless to deal with dangerous students; it did, however, deny school officials their former right to self-help, and directed that in the future the removal of disabled students could be accomplished only with the permission of the parents or, as a last resort, the courts.

As noted above, Congress passed the EHA after finding that school systems across the country had excluded one out of every eight disabled children from classes. In drafting the law, Congress was largely guided by the recent decisions in *Mills v. Board of Education of District of Columbia* and *PARC,* both of which involved the exclusion of hard-to-handle disabled students. *Mills* in particular demonstrated the extent to which schools used disciplinary measures to bar children from the classroom....

Congress attacked such exclusionary practices in a variety of ways. It required participating States to educate *all* disabled children, regardless of the severity of their disabilities, and included within the definition of handicapped those children with serious emotional disturbances. It further provided for meaningful parental participation in all aspects of a child's educational placement, and barred schools, through the stay-put provision, from changing that placement over the parents' objection until all review proceedings were completed. Recognizing that those proceedings might prove long and tedious, the Act's drafters did not intend to operate inflexibly and they therefore allowed for interim placements where parents and school officials are able to agree on one. Conspicuously absent from [the EHA], however, is any emergency exception for dangerous students. This absence is all the more telling in light of the injunctive decree issued in *PARC,* which permitted school officials unilaterally to remove students in extraordinary circumstances. Given the lack of any similar exception in *Mills,* and the close attention Congress devoted to these landmark decisions, we can only conclude that the omission was intentional; we are therefore not at liberty to engraft onto the statute an exception Congress chose not to create.

Our conclusion that [the EHA] means what it says does not leave educators hamstrung. The Department of Education has observed that, while the [child's] placement may not be changed [during any complaint proceeding], this does not preclude the agency from using its normal procedures for dealing with children who are endangering themselves or others. Such procedures may include the use of study carrels, timeouts, detention, or the restriction of privileges. More drastically, where a student poses an immediate threat to the safety of others, officials may temporarily suspend him or her for up to 10 school days. This authority, which respondent in no way disputes, not only ensures that school administrators can protect the safety of others by promptly removing the most dangerous of students, it also provides a cooling down period during which officials can initiate IEP review and seek to persuade the child's parents to agree to an interim placement. And in those cases in which the parents of a truly dangerous child adamantly refuse to permit any change in placement, the 10-day respite gives school officials an opportunity to invoke the aid of the courts under a provision in the IDEA that empowers courts to grant any appropriate relief.

Petitioner contends, however, that the availability of judicial relief is more illusory than real, because a party seeking review under [the EHA] must exhaust time-consuming administrative remedies, and because under the Court of Appeals construction of [the EHA's due process procedures], courts are as bound by the stay-put provision's automatic injunction as are schools. It is true that judicial review is normally not available under [the EHA] until all administrative proceedings are completed, but as we have previously noted, parents may bypass the administrative process where exhaustion would be futile or inadequate. While many of the EHA's procedural safeguards protect the rights of parents and children, schools can and do seek redress through the administrative review process, and we have no reason to believe that Congress meant to require schools alone to exhaust in all cases, no matter how exigent the circumstances. The burden in such cases, of course, rests with the school to demonstrate the futility or inadequacy of administrative review, but nothing in [the EHA] suggests that schools are completely barred from attempting to make such a showing. Nor do we think that [the EHA] operates to limit the equitable powers of district courts such that they cannot, in appropriate cases, temporarily enjoin a dangerous disabled child from attending school. As the EHA's legislative history makes clear, one of the evils Congress sought to remedy was the unilateral exclusion of disabled children by *schools,* not courts, and one of the purposes of [the EHA's procedural protections], therefore, was to prevent *school* officials from removing a child from the regular public school classroom over the parent's objection pending completion of the review proceedings. The stay-put provision in no way purports to limit or preempt the authority conferred on courts by [the EHA]; indeed, it says nothing whatever about judicial power.

In short, then, we believe that school officials are entitled to seek injunctive relief under [the EHA] in appropriate cases. In any such action, [the EHA's procedural protection] effectively creates a presumption in favor of the child's current educational placement which school officials can overcome only by showing that maintaining the child in his or her current placement is substantially likely to result in injury either to himself or herself, or to others. In the present case, we are satisfied that the District Court, in enjoining the state and local defendants from indefinitely suspending respondent or otherwise unilaterally altering his then current placement, properly balanced respondent's interest in receiving a free appropriate public education in accordance with the procedures and requirements of the EHA against the interests of the state and local school officials in maintaining a safe learning environment for all their students.

IV

We believe the courts below properly construed and applied [the EHA], except insofar as the Court of Appeals held that a suspension in excess of 10 school days does not constitute a change in placement. We therefore affirm the Court of Appeal's judgment on this issue as modified herein. . . .

Affirmed.

Resource D

Useful Education Law Web Sites

LEGAL SEARCH ENGINES

http://washlaw.edu
This Web site contains law-related sources on the Internet.

http://www.findlaw.com
FindLaw is an Internet resource that helps to find any Web site that is law related.

http://www.alllaw.com
AllLaw is another resource for locating law-related Web sites.

http://www.law.cornell.edu/
This is a Web site sponsored by Cornell Law School; it provides research and electronic publishing.

U.S. SUPREME COURT, FEDERAL COURTS, AND FEDERAL GOVERNMENT WEB SITES

http://www.supremecourtus.gov
This is the official Web site of the Supreme Court of the United States.

http://supct.law.cornell.edu/supct/index.html

This Web site contains recent decisions of the Supreme Court. It also has a free e-mail service that distributes the syllabi of the Court's decisions within hours after they are handed down.

http://thomas.loc.gov/

This Web site was prepared by the U.S. Library of Congress and has links to the federal court system.

http://www.uscourts.gov

This is the U.S. federal judiciary Web site.

http://www.gpoaccess.gov/fr/index.html

This Web site contains the *Federal Register.*

http://www.ed.gov/about/offices/list/ocr/index.html?src=mr

This is the Web site of the Office for Civil Rights.

http://www.house.gov/

This is the U.S. House of Representatives Web site.

http://www.senate.gov

This is the U.S. Senate Web site.

http://www.whitehouse.gov

This is the Web site of the White House.

http://www.ed.gov

This is the U.S. Department of Education Web site.

http://www.ed.gov/nclb/landing.jhtml?src=pb

This Web site contains the No Child Left Behind Act.

Resource E

Glossary of Terms, Acronyms, and Abbreviations

A.2d: Abbreviation for Atlantic Reporter, now in its second series, one of the regional reporters published by the West Group that contains state court decisions.

ADA (Americans with Disabilities Act): A civil rights statute prohibiting discrimination to individuals with disabilities in employment and programs.

Affirm: To uphold the decision of a lower court in an appeal.

Appeal: A resort to a higher court seeking review of a judicial action.

BIP (behavior intervention plan): Services and modifications to the educational program of a student with disabilities designed to address the student's behavioral difficulties. A BIP should include strategies for dealing with behaviors at the time they occur as well as long-term strategies for preventing future occurrences of misbehavior.

Cal.Rptr.3d: California Reporter, now in its third series, a compilation of state court decisions from California.

Cert.: Abbreviation for *certiorari,* a writ issued by an appeals court indicating that it will review a lower court's decision.

C.F.R. (Code of Federal Regulations): The set of regulations promulgated by various federal agencies to implement laws passed by Congress.

Civil rights: Personal rights guaranteed by the U.S. Constitution or a state constitution or by a federal or state statute.

Common law: The body of law that has developed as a result of court decisions, customs, and precedents.

EHCA (Education for All Handicapped Children Act): The original name of the Individuals with Disabilities Education Act. The law was originally passed in 1975, but the name was changed in 1990 to reflect current terminology.

EHLR: Abbreviation for Education of the Handicapped Law Reports an earlier version of the Individuals with Disabilities Education Law Reports, an unofficial compilation of court decisions, due process hearing decisions, and federal advisory letters now published by LRP Publications.

En banc (literally, "in the bench"): Indicates that a decision was issued by the full court of all appeals court judges in jurisdictions that have more than one panel of judges. En banc hearings are held when the judges feel that the issue is of particular significance or when requested by one of the parties and agreed to by the court.

Expulsion: A long-term exclusion from school, generally for disciplinary purposes; ordinarily, a disciplinary exclusion of more than 10 days is considered an expulsion.

F.3d: The abbreviation for the Federal Reporter, now in its third series. The Federal Reporter contains decisions of the federal circuit courts of appeal. The second series is abbreviated as F.2d.

FAPE (free appropriate public education): The educational program guaranteed by the Individuals with Disabilities Education Act for all students with disabilities. The standard—as enunciated by the U.S. Supreme Court in *Board of Education of the Hendrick Hudson Central School District v. Rowley* (458 U.S. 176 (1982)), its first case interpreting the IDEA's FAPE requirement—is that the educational program must both be developed in conformance with the statute's procedures and confer educational benefit.

FBA (functional behavioral assessment): An assessment of a student's overall behavior, including elements such as observations of the student that document aspects and types of behaviors; analysis of the situations that trigger misbehaviors; analysis of the effectiveness of interventions; medical, psychological, and social data that could impact student behavior; and any information that could provide insight into the student's behavior.

Fed. App'x: Abbreviation for Federal Appendix, a West Group unofficial publication that includes decisions of federal circuit courts of appeal that were not released for official publication.

F. Supp.2d: The abbreviation for the Federal Supplement, now in its second series. The Federal Supplement contains published decisions of federal trial or district courts. The first series was abbreviated as F. Supp.

IDEA (Individuals with Disabilities Education Act): The federal special education law, codified at 20 U.S.C. §§ 1400 *et seq.*

IDELR: Abbreviation for Individuals with Disabilities Education Law Reports, an unofficial compilation of court decisions, due process hearing decisions, and federal advisory letters published by LRP Publications.

IEP (individualized education program): A document outlining, among other things, the educational program and services a student with disabilities will receive in order to get a FAPE.

Independent hearing officer: An impartial third-party decision maker who conducts an administrative hearing and renders a decision on the merits of the dispute. In some jurisdictions hearing officers are known as administrative law judges.

Injunction: An equitable remedy, or court order, forbidding a party to take a contemplated action, restraining a party from continuing an action, or requiring a party to take some action.

In re (literally, "in the matter of"): Indicates that there are no adversarial parties in a judicial proceeding; this refers to the fact that a court is considering only a *res* ("thing"), not a person.

Interim alternative educational setting: An educational setting, other than the general education environment, where students may be temporarily placed for disciplinary reasons. In such a setting students should receive all of their usual educational services.

LEA: Abbreviation for local educational agency.

LRE (least restrictive environment): The placement that is as close as possible to a general education setting for a student with disabilities.

Manifestation review committee: A group charged with making the determination as to whether a student's misconduct was a manifestation of the student's disability. Generally a committee consists of members of the student's IEP team, other relevant school personnel, and the student's parents.

N.E.2d: Abbreviation for North Eastern Reporter, now in its second series, one of the regional reporters published by the West Group that contains state court decisions.

N.Y.S.2d: Abbreviation for New York Supplement, now in its second series, a compilation of decisions of state courts from New York.

N.W.2d: Abbreviation for North Western Reporter, now in its second series, one of the regional reporters published by the West Group that contains state court decisions.

OCR: Abbreviation for Office for Civil Rights, a federal agency within the Department of Education that deals with issues of discrimination.

On remand: This occurs when a higher court returns a case to a lower court with directions that the lower court take further action.

Opinion: A court's written explanation of its judgment.

OSEP: Abbreviation for Office of Special Education Programs, a division within the federal Department of Education's Office of Special Education and Rehabilitative Services that is charged with implementation of the IDEA.

OSERS: Abbreviation for Office of Special Education and Rehabilitative Services, a division within the federal Department of Education responsible for programs for individuals with disabilities of all ages.

P.3d: Abbreviation for Pacific Reporter, now in its third series, one of the regional reporters published by the West Group that contains state court decisions. The second series was abbreviated as P.2d.

Reevaluation: A complete and thorough reassessment of a student. Generally, all of the original assessments will be repeated, but additional assessments must be completed if necessary; the IDEA requires educators to reevaluate each child with a disability at least every three years.

Reverse: To revoke a lower court's decision in an appeal.

S. Ct.: The abbreviation for the Supreme Court Reporter, an unofficial compilation of Supreme Court opinions published by the West Group.

S.E.2d: Abbreviation for South Eastern Reporter, now in its second series, one of the regional reporters published by the West Group that contains state court decisions.

SEA: Abbreviation for State Educational Agency used in citations to designate state administrative hearing decisions.

So.2d: Abbreviation for Southern Reporter, now in its second series, one of the regional reporters published by the West Group that contains state court decisions.

Suspension: A short-term exclusion of a student from school, usually for less than 10 days, typically for disciplinary purposes.

S.W.3d: Abbreviation for South Western Reporter, now in its third series, one of the regional reporters published by the West Group that contains state court decisions.

U.S.: The abbreviation for the United States Reports, the official reporter of Supreme Court decisions.

U.S.C. (United States Code): The official compilation of statutes enacted by Congress.

Vacate: To set aside a lower court's decision in an appeal.

WL: Abbreviation for WestLaw, an online legal reporting system.

Index

CORWIN

A SAGE Company

The Corwin logo—a raven striding across an open book—represents the union of courage and learning. Corwin is committed to improving education for all learners by publishing books and other professional development resources for those serving the field of PreK–12 education. By providing practical, hands-on materials, Corwin continues to carry out the promise of its motto: **"Helping Educators Do Their Work Better."**